Pumpkin

A Super Food
for All 12 Months of the Year

DEEDEE STOVEL

Storey Publishing

The mission of Storey Publishing is to serve our customers by publishing practical information that encourages personal independence in harmony with the environment.

Edited by Andrea Dodge

Art direction and text design by Cynthia McFarland

Cover designed by Kent Lew

Illustration by © Scott Baldwin

Cover photography credits. Front, (top l. to r.) : © James Carrier Photography/Stockfood America, © Cazals-StockFood Munich/Stockfood America, © Eising FoodPhotography/Stockfood America, © Banderob-StockFood Munich/Stockfood America; (middle l. to r.) © Theresa Raffeto Photography/Stockfood America, © Cazals-StockFood Munich/Stockfood America, © Burke/Triolo Productions/Getty; (bottom l. to r.) © Bischof-StockFood Munich/Stockfood America, © Rick Mariani Photography/Stockfood America. Spine: © Burke/Triolo Productions/Getty.

Text production by Erin Dawson

Indexed by Andrea Chesman

Printed in the United States by CJK

10 9 8 7 6 5 4

LIBRARY OF CONGRESS CATALOGING-IN-PUBLICATION DATA

Stovel, DeeDee.
  Pumpkin : a super food for all 12 months of the year / by DeeDee Stovel.
    p. cm.
  Includes index.
  ISBN-13: 978-1-58017-594-4 (pbk. : alk. paper)
  1. Cookery (Pumpkin) I. Title.
TX803.P93S76 2005
641.6'562—dc22
                                                2005016483

Contents

Acknowledgments

Writing a cookbook is an act of love in large part because those you love and live with must eat your successes and failures. My husband Jack jokes that he gains 10 pounds for every cookbook I write. Fortunately there has been time in between for him to lose it. He has been my best critic and most supportive pal throughout the writing of this book, and for that I am most grateful. Our family's Sunday pizza nights were diverted into tasting sessions for various recipes thanks to the palates of Meg and Jezz, Dick and Lisa, Lennie, Molly and Emrich. Having eaters on hand is essential for a cookbook writer, and my new neighbors in California pitched right in. The next door Reidy family — Bill and Gina and their four kids, Chelsea, Olivia, Sam, and Elliot — took the job of tasting very seriously.

Recipe testers were invaluable for their careful testing and forthright commentary. Thanks especially to the stalwarts who kept coming back for more: Wendy Taylor, Donna Elefson, Judy Madden, Andy Shatken, Susan Smith, and Marcia Mallory. Thanks also to my daughters, Kate Stovel and Meg Holland; my brother and his wife, Dennis and Susan McCoy; my niece, Maura Kahn; and Sandy Jorling, Mimi Jorling, Polly Friedrichs, Larrie Rockwell, Kelly Martin, Lara Sellers, Becky Pettit, Mary Tierney, Joe Zeeman, Kimmie McCann, Jane Stuebner, Esther Christensen, Lynda Scofield, Pam Turton, and Pam Wakefield.

For ideas and inspiration I thank Barby Linnard. Judy Witts shared wonderful recipes. Dianne Cutillo, former editor at Storey Publishing, was most helpful and supportive in getting this project launched. Andrea Dodge, my editor, has been enthusiastic and encouraging throughout.

INTRODUCTION

My love affair with pumpkin began badly. As an aspiring ballerina longing for a tutu or, at the very least, a ballerina dress, my costume for the recital was puffy, not graceful, shiny and bright orange, not subtle and romantic. I was a pumpkin, not a twirling, leaping dancer in a lovely costume! It was the end of my ballet career, but not the end of the shiny orange costume my mom had lovingly sewn for me. The costume lived on in kid plays and for many Halloweens, until, no longer puffy or shiny, the limp and shredded orange satin was retired to the trash.

When my second daughter was born, my mom came up to help out. For some reason I have yet to fathom, my husband and I thought that helping with a baby, running after a two year old, and helping to run our house would not keep her busy enough. Since she was a wonderful cook and expert pie maker, and it was pumpkin season, we asked her to make a pumpkin pie from scratch. Only after we had wiped the last delicious crumbs from our lips did she tell us she always used canned pumpkins in her pies and had never before used a fresh pumpkin.

Things started to improve when this same daughter was a little older and needed her adenoids removed. We gave her a huge Teddy bear to take to the hospital. She promptly named the bear "Pumpkin" for reasons known only to her. A very worn and weary Pumpkin now sits on a big-girl bed and is much beloved by the new generation.

And here I am, many years later, riding on this family theme by chopping and peeling fresh pumpkins, opening can after can of prepared purée and becoming utterly fascinated with the versatility and flavor of pumpkin as an ingredient in all kinds of recipes. This amazing gourd, which appears in many cuisines and cultures around the world, has gotten my creative juices flowing, as you will see in the following pages.

Versatile PUMPKIN

When I told people I was writing a pumpkin cookbook, I got one of two reactions. "Ohhhh, I LOVE pumpkin, how exciting, when is it coming out?" or "You are writing about WHAT? Pumpkin? Why would you want to do that?" This book is clearly for the first group, but the second group will find there is a lot to love about pumpkins, clearly a super food!

Pumpkins happily grow in all climates across the United States. In fact, they grow on every continent except Antarctica. One of the many winter squashes, pumpkins have long been prized for their nutrition, adaptability, and staying power. The sturdy outer skin allows them to be stored in a cool place for months. Native to North America, pumpkins have been cultivated for about 9,000 years. For the indigenous people, pumpkin was a mainstay of their diet, and it has served as such for succeeding cultures. Pumpkin offers protein, complex carbohydrates, vitamin C, potassium, and huge amounts of vitamin A and beta-carotene, the precursor to vitamin A. It is high in fiber and low in calories. For sustenance, pumpkin is hard to beat.

Since pumpkin has been around for so long, and since it is found in cuisines across the globe, it is not surprising that pumpkin shows up in appetizers, soups, breads, dessert, salad, and savories of all kinds. It offers much more than the annual slice of pie at Thanksgiving, and I have by no means exhausted all the possibilities in this book. The mild, slightly sweet flavor lends itself to numerous ingredients. I had a great time adding pumpkin to my old favorite recipes, thinking up new combinations, and adapting ideas from other cultures. While in some cases the pumpkin flavor is almost too subtle to detect when used with strong, savory ingredients, it always adds texture, color, and nutrition. In other cases, the sweetness of pumpkin is the featured flavor, deepened by the addition of sugars and spices and leaving no doubt of its presence. A number of my recipe testers reported that they could not "taste" the pumpkin. True sometimes, but not a problem, because the lovely color is always there, as is the nutrition and the smooth texture.

Types of Pumpkins

Pumpkins are members of the gourd family, technically *cucurbitaceae*, affectionately known as cucurbits. The vines of this great family include hundreds of species, from cucumbers to melons to squash. Thin-skinned summer squash do not include pumpkin, which belongs in the category of thick-skinned winter squash. In some countries, pumpkin is a term used for all hard skinned squash. Of the many types of winter squash, pumpkin, butternut, acorn, hubbard, and buttercup are the most well-known and readily available. However, finding fresh pumpkin in markets during spring and summer is a bit of a challenge.

Pumpkin has a number of varieties, all of which are edible, but some are superior to others. The large ones that we carve into jack-o'-lanterns tend to be dry and stringy. Giant pumpkins, which may weigh over 1,000 pounds, follow suit. The original Halloween pumpkin is the Connecticut Field variety, which also makes a good pie. For the best eating, however, choose a denser, sweeter variety such as sugar or pie pumpkin; the pale-skinned Long Island cheese pumpkin; a delicious Japanese pumpkin known as Kabocha; bright orange French Red or Cinderella pumpkin;

elongated, yellowy orange banana pumpkin; dusky peachy Sonia pumpkin; tan to greenish Mexican pumpkin, or *calabaza*; or blue skinned Australian Queensland pumpkin. The names may change with the location, but taken together they form a subtly colored palate of the fall harvest that can be roasted, steamed, boiled, microwaved, grated, stuffed and served up in more ways than you can imagine.

There are cute little guys also, which are fun for decorating or using as little serving dishes when lightly roasted. Perfectly round baseball pumpkins, ribbed munchkins, Baby Bear, Jack be Little, or Baby Bo can mark places, fill a bowl, or decorate the hall table.

Cooking Pumpkin

FOR ALL METHODS, scrub the outside of the pumpkin before cooking and except for roasting whole or miniature pumpkins, pumpkins should be cut in half and the seeds removed. Pumpkin is done when the flesh is easily pierced with a fork.

METHOD	PREPARATION	EQUIPMENT	TEMPERATURE	TIME
Roast	Cut into large chunks; rub with oil WHOLE: Cut off top MINI: Leave whole	Roasting pan, lightly greased	400°F	45 minutes
Steam	Cut into wedges	4-quart saucepan with steamer basket	1 inch of water boiling on high heat	25–30 minutes
Boil	Cut into wedges	4-quart saucepan with cover	Boiling salted water over medium heat	20 minutes
Microwave	Cut into wedges	2-quart covered dish	High	5 minutes
Grill	Peel and cut into 1-inch chunks and rub with oil	Gas or charcoal grill	High	5 minutes on each side

Storing, Preparing, and Cooking Fresh Pumpkin

Many think of pumpkin as existing solely in dessert, especially in pie. In fact, pumpkin is a wonderful vegetable by itself in addition to being an adaptable ingredient in all kinds of savory dishes. It's mild flavor and soft texture when served with salt, pepper and a dab of butter provides a wonderful background to more highly seasoned poultry, meat, and fish.

Fresh pumpkins are abundant in the fall, but practically nonexistent in the market during winter, spring, and summer months. In the United States, most pumpkins are sold in the fall, when 99 percent of the crop is snatched up for jack-o'-lanterns and decorative pieces to create the harvest mood. The one exception I have found is the Japanese Kabocha pumpkin, which sits alongside butternut squash throughout the year. I find sugar, cheese, and Kabocha pumpkins the most satisfactory to use. If these are not available — it can be hard to get your hands on a fresh pumpkin once the supply of fall pumpkins is gone — butternut squash is an excellent substitute, with its smooth, creamy texture. It is reliably available in grocery stores everywhere throughout the year. The scarcity of fresh pumpkin after late fall or early winter is one reason to cook up entire pumpkins and store the leftovers in the freezer for late winter dishes.

Alternatively, keep whole fresh pumpkins during winter months by storing them in a dark, cool, dry place — not a refrigerator. A basement is perfect. For those without basements, store them outside and under cover from rain.

ADDING *Flavor*

Fresh and dried herbs as well as spices can perk up the mild flavor of pumpkin.

The herbs I choose to use with savory pumpkin dishes are: sage, thyme, rosemary, parsley (always use fresh because dried has no flavor), oregano, and marjoram.

Spices that lend themselves to pumpkin in savory dishes are: ginger, cumin, turmeric, chili powder, curry powders and pastes, whole cinnamon, whole cloves, and mustard.

Don't be limited by these lists. Add your own favorites!

Cutting and Peeling Pumpkin

Sugar pumpkins are the easiest to cut because of their small size. Wash the skin and, with a large knife, cut the pumpkin in half. Remove the stem. Scrape out the seeds and fibers with a large metal spoon and cook (see Cooking Pumpkin on page 5).

For large pumpkins, like the Long Island Cheese pumpkin, be sure to use a large, sharp chef's knife and a stable cutting board. Put a damp paper towel under the board to hold it in place. Slice a small amount from the bottom so the pumpkin won't wiggle while you cut. Start at the top and rock the knife back and forth as you cut the pumpkin in half from top to bottom. Remove the seeds and fibers and lay the cut sides on the board. Cut in quarters at least, or in smaller pieces if called for. Cook and peel as indicated in the recipe.

If a pumpkin is VERY hard to cut, you might try using a cleaver. If all else fails, throw the pumpkin on a concrete surface to smash it or at least crack it open, then use your knife. This is obviously a method of last resort, but it really works, especially if you can drop the pumpkin from a few steps. You may need to resort to such drastic measures if your pumpkin has been stored for several months because the skin becomes harder with time.

To peel an uncooked pumpkin, place the pumpkin cut-side down on a cutting board. With a sharp paring knife, cut the skin toward the bottom cut edge. Cut away from yourself. A potato peeler is not as satisfactory as a sharp knife. A cooked pumpkin is much easier to peel. For this reason, I include cooking instructions first in most recipes that use fresh pumpkin. When cool enough to handle, simply use a sharp paring knife to lift the skin from the pumpkin flesh.

> In general, 1 pound fresh pumpkin = 2 cups, peeled, cooked pumpkin = 2 cups cubes = 3–4 cups grated

When the Pumpkin Becomes the Serving Bowl

Heat the oven to 350°F. To prepare a small or mini pumpkin for individual servings, wash the skin, rub lightly with oil, and bake for 30 minutes, or until it is easily pierced with a fork. When cool enough to handle, cut a circle as you

Pumpkin's
Super Food Status

PUMPKIN IS NOT ONLY VERSATILE and tasty, it's good for you as well. Some doctors and nutritionists have identified pumpkin as a "super food," meaning that it is packed with rich phytonutrients that help protect the body and make for a healthier life. Steven Pratt, MD, author of the book *SuperFoods Rx: Fourteen Foods that Will Change Your Life,* includes pumpkin on his short list of nutrient-packed foods, noting that it is particularly helpful in protecting the skin from the damages of sunlight. So, a more youthful glow may be a side-benefit of incorporating pumpkin into your diet.

would for a jack-o'-lantern, about two inches from the stem. Remove the top and scrape out the seeds and fibers. Fill small pumpkins with salads, soups, risottos, puddings or whatever you fancy. They make nice individual serving bowls.

To prepare a large pumpkin for use as a serving bowl for soups and stews, choose a creamy Long Island cheese, a blue-skinned Queensland, or a bright orange Cinderella. Heat the oven to 350°F. Wash the pumpkin, cut off the top with a large knife and scoop out the seeds and fibers with a large metal spoon. Rub the inside and outside lightly with oil and place the pumpkin and top on a jelly-roll pan. Bake the pumpkin and top for 30 minutes. Remove the top and continue baking the bottom for 15 minutes longer, or until it can be pierced with a fork, but does not collapse. The pumpkin should be able to stand on its own.

Roasting Pumpkin

Preheat the oven to 400°F. Wash the pumpkin, cut in quarters, and remove the seeds and fibers. Rub the inside and outside with oil, and place the quarters in a roasting pan greased with oil, cut-side down. Roast for 45 minutes, or until the pumpkin is easily pierced with a fork and lightly caramelized. Allow it to cool slightly before removing the skin. Roast some sprigs of fresh herb, such as rosemary, sage, or thyme, with the pumpkin, and after peeling and mashing it, serve it as a side dish with salt, pepper, and butter. Add additional flavor by rubbing the cut sides with butter and maple syrup, or putting a little apple cider in the roasting pan.

Measure what you need and store the remainder for another recipe.

Microwaving Pumpkin

This is the quickest and simplest method for preparing small amounts of cooked pumpkin. Wash the pumpkin, remove the seeds and fibers, then cut the pumpkin into pieces that will fit in a microwave-safe covered dish. Add a tablespoon of water and cook on high for 5 minutes, or until easily pierced with a fork, up to 4 minutes longer. Let stand, covered, until cool enough to handle, then peel and proceed with your recipe.

Steaming Pumpkin

Wash pumpkin, remove the seeds and fibers, then cut the pumpkin into pieces. Place the pieces in a steamer basket over boiling water and steam for 20 to 30 minutes, or until easily pierced with a fork. Cool, remove the skin, and proceed with your recipe. Alternatively, peel before steaming.

Boiling Pumpkin

This is similar to steaming except that you will lose some of the water-soluble vitamins. Place the prepared pieces of pumpkin directly in boiling salted water and cook for 15 to 20 minutes, or until tender. Drain, cool, and peel.

Grating Pumpkin

Wash the pumpkin, remove the seeds and fibers, and then peel. Cut the pumpkin in eighths. Using a coarse metal grater, or a food processor, grate each piece. One-half pound will yield about 2 cups of grated pumpkin. Use in salads or baked goods, or quickly sauté as a vegetable.

Grilling Pumpkin

Wash the pumpkin, remove the seeds and fibers, peel, and cut into 1-inch chunks. Toss with olive oil and cook on a hot grill for 5 to 10 minutes, turning so all sides get browned. Season with salt and pepper and use in salads, or with grilled meat or poultry. You can

Pumpkin Capital
of the World

WHILE PUMPKIN FESTIVALS are numerous, the one dearest to my heart is in Half Moon Bay, California. This self-designated "Pumpkin Capital of the World" holds its Art and Pumpkin Festival on the weekend after Columbus Day. Pumpkin patches line the road for miles as one drives west toward this foggy Pumpkin Capital of the World, nestled behind high bluffs on the California coast. On weekends in October, the pumpkin patches are filled with families seeking the perfect pumpkin for their jack-o'-lantern.

The festival began in the early 1970s with some good citizens who wanted to beautify the town and celebrate its agricultural traditions. Today, the main street, lined with galleries, funky shops, and good restaurants, is indeed beautiful. And at this time of year, the fog is gone and the rains haven't yet arrived in the tiny coastal town, making the weather perfect to bring more than 200,000 to the festivities and the juried crafts fair.

Sounds from a lively country band grow louder as you approach the closed off main street, weaving through strollers, teens on clean-up crew, and happy wanderers. Soon the scent of chicken pumpkin grilled sausages hits you. Even though it is only ten in the morning, you can't resist a bite. Next to strike the taste buds is white chocolate pumpkin fudge, followed by a lick of pumpkin ice cream and a nibble of pumpkin cheesecake. For a break from eating, an endless parade of floats, decorated cars, witches, ghosts, and goblins of all ages marches down the main street followed at last by the prize-winning giant pumpkin, weighing in at more than 1,000 pounds. Nearby "Farmer Mike" carves amazing likenesses of the well-known on giant pumpkins using a professional array of chisels and knives. As the day winds down, a seat under a tree, a sip of beer or wine, and some good blue grass tunes make the perfect ending to a lively festival.

also toss the pumpkin with salad dressing or other marinades before grilling.

Puréeing Pumpkin

One pound of fresh pumpkin will yield about 1 cup of purée. Cook the pumpkin by one of the methods on page 5. Purée the pumpkin by mashing it with a potato masher, putting it through a ricer, or pulsing it in a food processor. Flavor with salt, pepper, and butter, or with herbs or spices, and enjoy a delightful side dish.

Toasting Pumpkin Seeds

Shelled pumpkin seeds are what I use in recipes in this book. When removing seeds from pumpkins, you will find they are covered with a tough white shell. Some will tell you to bake them, salt them, and eat them as a snack. I have never enjoyed the end result of this, even though it appeals to my frugal, "waste not, want not" side. I much prefer the green hulless ones, which are also called pepitas. When toasted, they make a delightful, crunchy, nutritious snack or a great addition to many recipes.

To make 1 cup of toasted pumpkin seeds, toss one cup of raw seeds with 1 teaspoon oil and a little salt. Heat a toaster oven to 300°F. Toast for 5 to 7 minutes, or until the seeds swell, become golden, and make a popping sound. Don't let them get dark, or they will turn bitter. Eat as a snack; use as a topping for salads, casseroles, or crusts for meat and fish; or mix with other seeds, nuts, cereals, or pretzels for a party mix.

An alternative method is to heat the oil in a skillet, add the seeds and cook for 2 to 3 minutes, until the seeds start popping and lightly brown.

Storing Leftover, Cooked Pumpkin

Cooked fresh pumpkin will keep in the refrigerator for a week. Otherwise, place it in a plastic freezer bag in small batches and freeze for up to 3 months. Use in recipes that call for cooked pumpkin.

Transfer leftover canned pumpkin to a covered container, store in the refrigerator for up to a week, and add it to your favorite recipes. It will keep in the freezer for several months.

Recipes for Every Style and Part of Pumpkin

Famous Pumpkin
Festivals

MORTON, ILLINOIS, home to the Libby's branch of Nestle and site of its canned pumpkin processing plant, declares itself a world pumpkin capital (see Pumpkin Capital of the World, page 10), and since the late 1960s, holds an annual Pumpkin Festival with a huge parade and carnival. Catapults and numerous inventive hurling devices draw the biggest crowds to witness the famous "punkin" chucking" contest, which we can only imagine.

Pumpkintown, South Carolina, an early settlement named after the huge pumpkins that grew in the rich soil of nearby fields, needs mentioning. Their annual festival features a band and float parade along with good southern food, including pumpkin pies.

For the "Decorated Pumpkin Capital of the World," we turn to DeKalb City, Illinois, where the courthouse lawn is filled with decorated pumpkins at its annual festival.

Harvest time is May down under, when the town of Goomeri, Australia, holds its annual pumpkin festival. The town is also home to a pie shop called the "Pumpkin Pie," with pies made by Patsy, the "pie-ologist."

STARTERS, SNACKS *and* BEVERAGES

CHAPTER 2

*W*ho would have thought of drinking pumpkin or beginning a meal with pumpkin? In this chapter you will find many ways to do both. Dips, twists, and trail mixes with crunchy pumpkins are a few ways to nibble on pumpkin. A pumpkin spiced latte? A martini spiked with pumpkin? You may be surprised with what you find in this chapter.

STARTERS & SNACKS

Savory Pumpkin

MANY THINK OF PIE and desserts as the place to add pumpkin. Pumpkin travels the world from Africa to Australia to Asia to North, South, and Central America, where it is found in savory soups, stews, grain dishes, and just about anything else one can think of. It adds depth and richness to beef, lamb, pork, and chicken, as well as fish. It brightens pasta, rice, polenta, and many other grains with color and subtle flavor. Parsley, sage, rosemary, and thyme are not just the herbs of song, they are great companions to pumpkin. Many wonderful recipes follow, but you can add leftover roasted, steamed, fresh or canned pumpkin and some of these herbs to practically any recipe, and you will not be disappointed.

WHEN YOU ARE LOOKING for a crunchy alternative to nuts, there is nothing better than puffed up pepitas, otherwise known as shelled pumpkin seeds. When roasted or toasted they puff and pop, making them a perfect ingredient to add to trail mixes and salads or as a crunchy topping to many dishes. By themselves they make great munching. Puréed pumpkin lends its creamy texture to dips and cheesy mixtures. Spicy little chunks of pumpkin tucked into toasted wonton cups make tasty one-bite morsels at cocktail parties. Choose from among these snacks and starters and also try adding pumpkin to some of your favorite recipes to change the flavor and texture and to give a nutritional boost.

Black Bean Dip

A smooth creamy texture with a bit of chunkiness, a deep rich flavor, and bright hints of cilantro make this fresh-tasting bean dip a favorite on the hors d'oeuvre table.

MAKES 4 CUPS

1 tablespoon canola oil

1–2 jalapeño chiles (seeds and membranes removed), minced

½ cup green bell pepper, chopped

1 medium onion, chopped (about 1 cup)

3 cloves garlic, minced

3 cups cooked black beans, rinsed and drained

1 cup canned unsweetened pumpkin

3 tablespoons fresh lime juice

1 teaspoon ground cumin

½ teaspoon salt

2–3 tablespoons water

¼ cup finely chopped cilantro, plus one sprig

Assorted corn chips and vegetables

1 Heat the oil in a medium skillet. Cook the peppers and onion over medium heat for about 3 minutes, until they soften slightly. Add the garlic and cook another minute. Set aside.

2 Place the beans, pumpkin, lime juice, cumin, salt, and water in the bowl of a food processor and purée until partially smooth, stirring with a scraper as needed. Add the onion, peppers, garlic, and the cilantro and pulse a few times until blended but not completely smooth.

3 Scrape the dip into a bowl, garnish with the sprig of cilantro, and serve with corn chips and vegetables, such as a mix of white, blue, and yellow tortilla chips; baby carrots; and slices of red bell pepper.

Holiday Pumpkin Dip

MAKES 2 CUPS

Every Christmas, my nieces Kristen and Betsy make this creamy dip, flavored with beef and Mexican spices and dotted with bits of red and green pepper. Serve with thin slices from a long, skinny baguette.

8 ounces cream cheese, softened

½ cup canned unsweetened pumpkin

1 clove garlic, minced

2 tablespoons minced fresh onion

1 teaspoon ground cumin

1 teaspoon chili powder

⅓ cup minced dried beef (see Note)

¼ cup chopped green bell pepper

⅓ cup chopped red bell pepper

2 tablespoons lime juice

2 tablespoons minced fresh cilantro

1 long, skinny baguette, thinly sliced on the diagonal

1 Beat together the cream cheese, pumpkin, garlic, onion, cumin, and chili powder until smooth and creamy.

2 Stir in the beef, green and red peppers, and lime juice. Spoon into a small, pretty bowl, sprinkle with cilantro, and chill.

NOTE: Dried beef can be found in jars on supermarket shelves or packaged in the deli section.

Pumpkin-Shaped
Cheeseball

For a retro look to your party table, you definitely need a cheese ball. Instead of a sphere rolled in nuts, here is a pumpkin dusted in paprika and adorned with a pepper stem.

SERVES 12–16

2 cups grated sharp orange Cheddar

1 cup small curd cottage cheese

8 ounces cream cheese, softened

3/4 cup crumbled blue cheese

1 tablespoon Worcestershire sauce

Dash of cayenne pepper

Paprika

1 strip of green bell pepper

Assorted crackers

1 Place the Cheddar, cottage cheese, cream cheese, blue cheese, Worcestershire, and cayenne in the bowl of a food processor, and process until well blended.

2 Wrap the mixture in plastic wrap and refrigerate for at least 2 hours.

3 While still wrapped in plastic, roughly shape into a ball and set on a cutting board. Refine the shape, and remove the plastic wrap. With the handle of a knife, indent lines from top to bottom to resemble a pumpkin. Sprinkle the entire ball with paprika and carefully move to a large serving plate.

4 Place the pepper strip on top and surround the ball with simple crackers.

Herbed Parmesan Twists

Frozen puff pastry is a dream for party givers. It is almost as good as what you would literally spend hours creating, and its versatility is endless. These twists are but one simple way to create an appetizer in moments. Allow the frozen pastry to sit out for half an hour before using, and you will find a most pliant companion that can be rolled, twisted, and shaped anyway you want.

MAKES 28 TWISTS

PASTRY

- 1 sheet frozen puff pastry, thawed for 30 minutes
- 1 egg
- 1 tablespoon water

FILLING

- ½ cup freshly grated Parmesan
- ¼ cup canned unsweetened pumpkin
- 1 tablespoon minced fresh parsley
- ½ teaspoon ground cumin
- Dash of cayenne
- ¼ teaspoon salt

1 Heat the oven to 400°F.

2 Roll the dough on a lightly floured surface into an 8 by 16-inch rectangle. Cut in half lengthwise to make two 4-inch-wide pieces. Beat the egg with the water in a small bowl and brush both pieces with some of the egg mixture.

3 To make the filling, combine all the ingredients, except 2 tablespoons of the Parmesan, in a medium bowl. Spread the filling on one piece of the egg-brushed dough and top with the other, egg-side down. Roll the top lightly, being careful not to let the filling ooze out. Trim any ragged edges.

4 Cut into 28 pieces, about ¾-inch each. Twist each piece, brush with the remaining egg, sprinkle with the remaining Parmesan, and set on an ungreased baking sheet.

5 Bake for 10 minutes, or until lightly golden. Serve warm.

Thai Curried Pumpkin in Phyllo Cups

Inspiration for these delightful little mouthfuls comes from twin sisters Mary Barber and Sara Whitehead, who operate a catering business in San Francisco. Smooth with a little crunch and a small kick, these darlings will not last long. Thai green curry paste can be found in the Asian section of the supermarket either in a jar or a package.

MAKES 36 CUPS

PASTRY

4 sheets phyllo dough, stacked, cut into 2½-inch squares, and covered loosely with plastic wrap

Butter-flavored spray

FILLING

1 pound fresh Japanese Kabocha pumpkin, seeded (about 1½ cups cooked)

¼ cup mango chutney

¼ cup coconut milk

2 tablespoons chunky peanut butter

1 tablespoon minced fresh cilantro

1 tablespoon fresh lime juice

¼–½ teaspoon Thai green curry paste

TOPPING

3 tablespoons chopped salted peanuts

1 Heat the oven to 350°F.

2 Place 2 or 3 squares of phyllo in 36 miniature muffin cups. Spray the insides and edges with the butter-flavored spray and bake for 6 to 7 minutes, or until the cups are lightly browned. Cool on a wire rack and then remove from muffin cups.

3 Boil the pumpkin in water in a medium saucepan for 15 to 20 minutes, or until easily pierced with a fork. The skin will easily peel off. Cut the pumpkin into ¼-inch cubes and let cool. You will need 1½ cups.

4 Combine the chutney, coconut milk, peanut butter, cilantro, lime juice, and curry paste in a medium bowl. Stir in the cooled pumpkin. Fill each little cup with a teaspoon of the curried pumpkin and sprinkle with the chopped peanuts. It is best to fill these shortly before serving. This recipe can be easily doubled.

Pumpkin Butter

MAKES ¾ CUP

This spicy spread is a delightful change from super sweet jam for your morning toast. Pack it in a pretty jar and bring it along as a host gift. Instead of using plain unsweetened pumpkin, use this blend in sweet recipes.

2 cups canned unsweetened pumpkin

⅔ cup brown sugar

1 tablespoon fresh lemon juice

1 teaspoon grated lemon zest

¼ teaspoon ground allspice

¼ teaspoon ground cinnamon

¼ teaspoon ground ginger

⅛ teaspoon ground cloves

1 Combine all the ingredients in a medium saucepan and cook over medium-low heat for 20 to 30 minutes, until thickened and darkened. Stir regularly while cooking.

2 Cool and store in a glass jar in the refrigerator for several weeks.

Giant Pumpkin CONTESTS

Giant pumpkins are getting bigger every year, as attested to by the World Pumpkin Confederation, which sponsors official weigh-off contests at pumpkin festivals in the United States, Canada, and Australia. Among the strict rules governing these official contests, pumpkins must be creamy yellow to orange. The confederation was formed in 1983 to promote giant pumpkin growing, and now there are members from more than 30 countries and a myriad of officially sanctioned weigh-off contests.

Pumpkin Chutney

MAKES 1½
PINTS, THREE
1-CUP CANNING
JARS

Chutney is a delightful condiment to serve with curries and grilled meats. It makes a tasty topping on cream cheese to serve with crackers or atop a thick slice of sharp cheddar for hors d'oeuvres.

1½ pounds fresh pumpkin, seeds and fibers removed, peeled, and cut into ½-inch chunks (3 cups)

2 cups cider vinegar

¾ cup dark brown sugar

½ cup water

1 medium onion, thinly sliced

1 jalapeño chile, minced

¼ cup currants

8 whole cloves

1½ tablespoons peeled and grated fresh ginger

1 tablespoon molasses

1 tablespoon balsamic vinegar

1 cinnamon stick

1 teaspoon salt

½ teaspoon dry mustard

1 Sterilize three 8-ounce canning jars and lids by washing them in a dishwasher or placing them in a kettle filled with water and gently boiling them for 20 minutes.

2 Place all of the ingredients in a large, heavy-bottomed saucepan over medium-high heat. Bring to a boil, reduce the heat, and cook, uncovered, for 30 to 45 minutes, stirring often, until the pumpkin is tender and the chutney is syrupy.

3 Using a slotted spoon, loosely pack the chutney into the clean jars, pour the syrup in the jars until it flows over the top, seal, and let sit on the counter for a week before using.

Pepita Party Mix

Not only is this crunchy mix impossible to stop eating, it is healthful. For an alternative, add a cup of unsalted peanuts or cashew pieces. People of all ages love it. Moms and dads trying to get their children to eat healthful snacks can keep a big tin handy.

MAKES 5 CUPS

3 tablespoons unsalted butter

2 cups shelled pumpkin seeds (pepitas)

2 cups small, square wheat cereal

1 cup broken pretzel sticks

3 cloves garlic, minced

½ teaspoon ground cumin

1 teaspoon salt (sea salt, if available)

1 Heat the oven to 300°F.

2 Place the butter in a roasting pan and bake in the oven until the butter melts. Add the pepitas, cereal, pretzels, garlic, cumin, and salt, and stir until everything glistens with melted butter.

3 Bake for 30 to 35 minutes, or until the pepitas swell and "pop," and the garlic becomes fragrant.

4 Place the pan on a wire rack and cool completely before packing the mix in an airtight container for up to a month, if it lasts that long.

Pumpkin Seed Gorp

Knowing a little bag of gorp is in my backpack has always made the steep parts of a hike bearable. The trouble with gorp is knowing when you have had enough. For some of us, that is very difficult. There are many ways to put together this traditional hiking mix. Any combination of dried fruit, nuts, and a bit of chocolate will do. It provides a burst of energy to the weary hiker.

MAKES 3 CUPS

1 cup shelled, roasted and salted pumpkin seeds (pepitas)

1 cup roasted cashews

½ cup dried cranberries

½ cup semi-sweet chocolate chips

1 Toss everything together in a small bowl. Take on hikes, or enjoy as a snack.

2 Store in an airtight container for up to a month.

Pepitas (SHELLED PUMPKIN SEEDS)

Pepitas are pumpkin seeds with the outer hull removed that can be purchased raw or toasted and salted in supermarkets, Mexican markets, and whole food markets. When toasted, they swell and pop and become a wonderful crunchy snack, especially if mixed with a little oil, salt, and spices. If toasted for more than 5 minutes, they become bitter and quickly lose their appeal.

Pepitas pack a nutritional wallop for a snack food. Relatively low in fat and rich in protein, zinc, antioxidants, vitamin E, iron, phosphorus, and fiber, these little seeds are hard to beat and even harder to stop eating.

Spicy Pepita Nuts

Pepitas, pine nuts, pistachios, and almonds are baked together with butter and mildly hot spices to make a crunchy mix. Serve at a cocktail party. Pack in snack bags for lunches.

MAKES 5 CUPS

1½ cups raw shelled pumpkin seeds (pepitas)

¾ cup pine nuts

¾ cup shelled pistachios

½ cup whole almonds

¼ cup sugar

1 teaspoon salt

¼–½ teaspoon cayenne

3 tablespoons unsalted butter

1 Heat the oven to 300°F.

2 Combine the pepitas, pine nuts, pistachios, almonds, sugar, salt, and cayenne in a large bowl.

3 Line a jelly-roll pan with aluminum foil, spray with cooking spray, and spread the nut mixture in the pan. Dot the top with the butter and bake for 30 to 40 minutes, stirring every 10 minutes, until the butter is melted and the nuts are glazed and lightly browned.

4 Cool on a rack, stirring occasionally. Pack in an airtight container for up to two weeks.

Black Bean Quesadillas

Cilantro and black beans combine again for a tasty alternative to chips and salsa. These tidbits can also serve as a light lunch or supper when accompanied with a crisp salad. Make Grated Candied Pumpkin (page 60) with excess pumpkin.

MAKES 20 PIECES

1 tablespoon canola oil

1 small onion, chopped (about ½ cup)

1 jalapeño chile, seeded, membranes removed, minced

½ green bell pepper, seeded, membranes removed, chopped (about ¼ cup)

½ pound fresh pumpkin, seeds and fibers removed, peeled and grated (about 1 cup)

¼ cup canned unsweetened pumpkin

2 cups cooked black beans, or one 15-ounce can, rinsed and drained

1 teaspoon chili powder

1 teaspoon ground cumin

1 teaspoon salt

10 fresh 5-inch corn tortillas

5 ounces sharp Cheddar, grated (about 2½ cups)

10 tablespoons chopped fresh cilantro

1 Heat the oven to 375°F.

2 Heat the oil in a large skillet over medium heat. Cook the onion for 2 to 3 minutes until they soften. Add the chile, pepper, and fresh pumpkin and continue to cook 5 minutes longer, stirring occasionally.

3 Add the canned pumpkin, beans, chili powder, cumin, and salt. Slightly mash the beans with a potato masher and continue to cook and stir until mixture is well blended.

4 Place 5 of the tortillas on a large cookie sheet. Divide the filling among them and sprinkle each with ½ cup of the cheese and 2 tablespoons of the cilantro. Place a tortilla on top of each and gently press down with the palm of your hand.

5 Bake for 15 minutes, or until the tortillas are lightly toasted, but not too crisp, and the cheese is melted. Cut each stack in quarters and serve as appetizers or hors d'oeuvres.

BEVERAGES

PUMPKINS ARE VERSATILE. Drinking them may not be the first thing that comes to mind, but think of adding color, nutrition, and texture to drinks — not to mention the mild flavor.

Pumpkin Martini

Pumpkin martini was a fall feature in the entertaining section of the *San Francisco Chronicle*. It features Bols Pumpkin Smash liqueur and rum. None of these ingredients sing out martini to me, but for those ever on the lookout for something new, it is worth a try. Add a little spice and a dash of cream.

Mulled Pumpkin Beer

Pumpkin ale is available in the fall, and those who make beer will sometime create a batch. While purist beer lovers my turn up their noses at this travesty, add a cinnamon stick, some whole cloves, and allspice and gently warm the mixture for a spicy drink perfect for a crisp fall day. Serve it in mugs garnished with a lemon peel.

For actually brewing up a batch of pumpkin beer, refer to David Ruggiero's Skinny Puppy Pumpkin Beer in *The Perfect Pumpkin* by Gail Damerow.

Pumpkin Latte

In the fall, coffee shops may offer Pumpkin Latte. Milk is a natural with pumpkin, especially when sweetened and spiced. Start with a shot of espresso, mix it with several tablespoons canned unsweetened pumpkin, a teaspoon of sugar, and 1/4 teaspoon of the spices of your choice. I would suggest cinnamon, with a pinch of nutmeg. Fill up the mug with steamed milk, and voila!

Here's a tip for quickly steaming milk. Fill mug 3/4 full and microwave on high for 30 seconds. Use an aerating tool to froth the milk, and then pour into the espresso.

Pumpkin Blizzard

Mix canned unsweetened pumpkin with spices, vanilla ice cream, and a little milk, whirl in a blender, and enjoy a great milkshake.

Mango Pumpkin
Smoothie

Sweet and spicy with a touch of tang combine with subtle pumpkin to make this a smoothie to remember. Be creative and concoct a mix with your favorite fruits and flavors.

SERVES 2

1 cup mango juice, or other 100 percent fruit juice

1 cup nonfat vanilla yogurt

⅓ cup canned unsweetened pumpkin

1 ripe mango, peeled and cut into 1-inch chunks, or 1 cup frozen mango pieces

1 tablespoon sugar

¼ teaspoon ground cinnamon

⅛ teaspoon ground nutmeg

4 ice cubes

1 Place all the ingredients in the jar of a blender and purée until smooth.

2 Taste and adjust the flavorings.

3 Serve icy cold.

Orange-Banana
Smoothie

SERVES 2

Banana, pumpkin, and yogurt combine into the smoothest of smoothies, brightened with orange for a perfect way to begin the day.

1 cup orange juice

1 cup nonfat vanilla yogurt

⅓ cup canned unsweetened pumpkin

1 banana, peeled and cut into 1-inch chunks

1 tablespoon sugar

¼ teaspoon ground cinnamon

⅛ teaspoon ground nutmeg

4 ice cubes

1 Place all the ingredients in the jar of a blender and purée until smooth.

2 Taste and adjust the flavorings.

3 Serve icy cold.

SOUPS *and* SALADS

*P*ut a hearty soup together with a light salad and a nice loaf of bread, and you have created a simple but satisfying meal for yourself and your family or friends. One of the great things about soup is that you can make a big pot of it to have again and again. Pumpkin soups and salads are packed with those vegetables that are so good for you and so tasty and colorful. It is definitely a win/win combination.

Creating soups with pumpkin or adding it to old favorites could have been an endless project. Every combination I could think of ended up as a soup I would love to serve to my friends. Chunks of fresh pumpkin and pumpkin purée add flavor, color, texture and nutrition. The adaptability of pumpkin sings out from soup pot to soup pot.

Pumpkin brightens the color palette of winter salads when tossed with dark green and purple leaves. Crunchy pepitas spark the softer greens and fruits of summer salads. The nutty sweetness of pumpkin seed oil enhances any salad. Add it to your stable of oils to sprinkle over salads along with good quality wine vinegars and balsamics.

Jack-o'-Lantern

As the Irish legend goes, many years ago in Ireland, Jack, a sly and deceitful drunkard who had tricked the devil several times, died. Because of his wayward life, he was not admitted to Heaven. Because of his deals with the devil, he couldn't go to Hell and was doomed to wander throughout the land in darkness until Judgment Day. The devil tossed him a hot coal, which Jack put in a turnip to light his way and ever since, Jack of the Lantern has been the symbol of the damned/lost soul.

Roasted Ginger Pumpkin– *Pear Soup*

My basic fall soup makes a wonderful lunch all by itself and, when accompanied by a nice salad and a good loaf of bread, makes supper or lunch. Without the addition of half and half, the soup is smooth and tasty. The cream adds a richness which is nice, but not necessary.

SERVES 6

1½ pounds fresh pumpkin, seeds and fibers removed, cut into big chunks

1 tablespoon olive oil, plus extra for brushing on pumpkin

1 tablespoon butter

½ cup chopped onion

2 tablespoons minced shallots

2 teaspoons peeled and grated fresh ginger

1 teaspoon salt

1–2 red or green ripe Anjou pears, peeled, cored, and cut in chunks

4 cups chicken broth, homemade if possible

½ cup half-and-half (optional)

NOTE: Peeling raw pumpkin is not easy; cooked pumpkin is much simpler (see page 7). A friend of mine who loves pumpkin roasts it and uses it in soup, peel and all. She says it is delicious.

1 Heat the oven to 400°F.

2 Brush each pumpkin chunk with oil. Bake for 45 minutes, or until easily pierced with a fork. When cool enough to handle, peel, mash, and measure 3 cups. Store the rest in the refrigerator for up to a week, or in the freezer for up to 3 months.

3 Heat the oil and butter in a large saucepan over medium heat for 1 minute. Add the onion and shallots and cook for about 5 minutes, or until translucent, stirring occasionally. Add 1 teaspoon of the ginger, the salt, and the pumpkin. Cook for another minute until warm.

4 Add the pear and broth and cook for about 20 minutes, until the pear is easily pierced with a fork. Stir in the remaining teaspoon of ginger.

5 In small batches, purée the soup in a blender or with a hand-held blender in the saucepan, until the consistency is smooth and creamy.

6 Return the soup to the saucepan and add half-and-half, if desired. Gently heat, but do not boil. Serve hot.

Caribbean Black Bean
Pumpkin Soup

A velvety rich, spicy soup that is a meal in itself. Gather friends by the fire on a cold and rainy night with steaming bowls of this soup and crusty bread for a perfect cozy evening.

SERVES 8

1 tablespoon canola oil

1 large onion, chopped (about 1½ cups)

2 cloves garlic, minced

2 teaspoon ground cumin, plus more to taste

1 teaspoon salt, plus more to taste

Dash cayenne, plus more to taste

3 cups cooked black beans, or one and a half 15-ounce cans, rinsed and drained

1 can (14.5 ounces) whole tomatoes with juice

2 tablespoons canned green chiles or, for more heat, 2 fresh serrano chiles, seeded and minced

4 cups vegetable or chicken broth

2 cups canned unsweetened pumpkin

¼ cup chopped fresh cilantro

⅓ cup sour cream

1 Heat the oil in a Dutch oven or soup pot over medium heat for 1 minute. Add the onion and cook for several minutes, stirring, until onion begins to soften. Add the garlic, cumin, salt, and cayenne and cook until fragrant and well mixed, about 3 minutes.

2 Purée the beans, tomatoes, and chiles in a blender until smooth and creamy. Add the onion mixture to the blender and continue puréeing until incorporated. If necessary, moisten with a little broth.

3 Return the soup to the pot and add the broth and pumpkin. Taste and season with more salt, cumin, or cayenne to taste. Cook over medium-low heat for 20 minutes, stirring occasionally. Taste again and adjust the seasonings, if desired.

4 Ladle the soup into bowls and garnish with the cilantro and sour cream.

NOTE: Green chiles are quite mild and are available in cans, either whole or chopped. Serrano chiles are hot, though by no means the hottest, and must be purchased fresh. They are small and green and, as with all hot chiles, the heat is centered in the ribs and seeds. Carefully scrape these away for a milder flavor.

Southwest Chicken
Pumpkin Soup

SERVES 6

This colorful soup can be made with leftover cooked chicken and is a great opportunity to use any roasted pumpkin that is stored in your freezer.

½ pound fresh pumpkin, seeds and fibers removed, cut into chunks

1 tablespoon olive oil, plus extra for brushing chunks

1 large onion, thinly sliced (about 1½ cups)

2 cloves garlic, minced

1 small red bell pepper, seeded and chopped

1 pound boneless skinless chicken breast halves or thighs, cut into ½-inch chunks

2 teaspoons ground cumin

1 teaspoon salt, plus more to taste

¼ teaspoon hot pepper flakes
Freshly ground black pepper

1 tablespoon tomato paste

4 cups chicken broth

1 cup frozen corn kernels

1–2 tablespoons freshly squeezed lime juice

1 tablespoon chopped fresh cilantro

1 Heat the oven to 400°F. Brush each pumpkin chunk with oil. Bake for 45 minutes, or until the pumpkin is easily pierced with a fork. Cool slightly and peel. Measure out 1 cup and mash. Store the rest in the refrigerator for up to a week, or freeze it for up to 3 months.

2 Heat the oil in a Dutch oven or soup pot over medium heat for 1 minute. Add the onion and cook for several minutes until they begin to wilt. Add the bell pepper and garlic and continue cooking and stirring for a few more minutes until softened.

3 While the vegetables are cooking, mix the chicken in a small bowl with the cumin, salt, pepper flakes, and a few grinds of black pepper.

4 Add the chicken mixture to the onion mixture and cook for about 5 minutes, until the aromas rise from the pot as the chicken begins to cook. Stir in the pumpkin and tomato paste and cook for several minutes, until well blended. Add the broth and corn, bring to a boil, reduce the heat, and simmer, uncovered, for 5 to 15 minutes, until the chicken is tender and no longer pink.

5 Season with the lime juice, taste, and add more salt if needed. Ladle into soup bowls and garnish with cilantro.

Lentil-Pumpkin Soup
with Spinach

Our star ingredient perks up this hearty favorite with a touch of color, some smoothness, and a nutritional burst. Serve piping hot with a country loaf and a salad of field greens.

SERVES 8

2 cups French green lentils (or regular brown lentils)

1 tablespoon olive oil

2 stalks celery, chopped (about ½ cup)

1 medium onion, chopped (1 cup)

1 carrot, peeled and chopped (about ¾ cup)

1 clove garlic, minced

½ pound smoked sausage, such as kielbasa, cut in ¼-inch slices

1 teaspoon salt

Freshly ground black pepper

1 teaspoon dried thyme

6 cups vegetable broth or water

1 cup canned whole plum tomatoes

1½ cups canned unsweetened pumpkin

1 tablespoon brown sugar

1 tablespoon fresh lemon juice

2 tablespoons red wine vinegar

4 cups washed fresh baby spinach

1 Rinse and pick over the lentils.

2 Heat the oil in a Dutch oven or soup pot over medium heat for 1 minute. Add the celery, onion, carrots, and garlic. Sauté for about 7 minutes, stirring occasionally, until the vegetables begin to wilt, soften, and caramelize. Stir in the sausage slices and cook until they begin to brown, another 5 minutes. Season with the salt, pepper to taste, and thyme.

3 Place the lentils and broth in the pot, bring to a boil, reduce the heat, cover, and simmer for 30 minutes, or until the lentils are tender.

4 Cut the tomatoes in half and add them and their juices to the pot along with the pumpkin, brown sugar, lemon juice, and vinegar. Cook, covered, for about 15 minutes longer, to give the flavors a chance to blend. Taste and adjust the seasonings. Add water if the soup seems too thick.

5 Just before serving, add the spinach and simmer only until the spinach is wilted, but still bright green.

Mushroom-Pumpkin Soup

For mushroom lovers, this deeply satisfying, earthy soup is full of subtle and interesting flavor and textures. With a loaf of crusty bread and a salad of warm, wilted winter greens, you have the perfect cold weather supper.

SERVES 6

- ¾ ounce (¾ cup) dried wild mushrooms, porcini if possible
- ¾ cup hot water
- 1 tablespoon unsalted butter
- 1 tablespoon canola or grapeseed oil
- ¾ pound white button mushrooms, cleaned, trimmed and sliced
- ½ cup (1 large) shallots, minced
- ¼ cup medium-dry sherry
- 1 teaspoon salt
- ¼ teaspoon dried thyme
- 3–3½ cups chicken broth, homemade if possible, or two 14½-ounce cans
- 1½ cup (15 ounces) canned unsweetened pumpkin
- 1 cup heavy cream

1 Soak the dried mushrooms in a small bowl with ¾ cup hot water for 15 minutes. Strain, save the liquid, and chop the mushrooms.

2 Heat the butter and oil in a large skillet over medium heat until the butter bubbles. Add the prepared dried mushrooms, white button mushrooms, and shallots and cook over medium-low heat until the fresh mushrooms give off their liquid and shrink in size, about 5 to 10 minutes. Add the sherry, season with the salt and thyme, and continue cooking until the aromas rise from the pan and most of the liquid is gone, about 3 minutes.

3 Add enough chicken broth to the reserved mushroom liquid to make 4 cups. Pour about half of this into a blender and add the mushroom mixture. Purée until smooth.

4 In a large saucepan, combine the puréed mushrooms, remaining broth, and pumpkin. Bring to a boil over medium heat, reduce the heat, and simmer for 15 minutes. Taste and adjust the seasoning, if desired.

5 Add the cream and gently heat through without boiling. Serve immediately.

Creamy Kale Pumpkin Soup

Kale packs a nutritional wallop that is hard to beat. Pumpkin makes it even better. But the best part of this winter soup is its mild and smooth pumpkin potato flavor, spiked with a bitter hint of kale. Serve with a zesty sourdough bread for a wonderful winter lunch or supper.

SERVES 6

3 slices bacon

1 tablespoon olive oil

1 medium onion, chopped (1 cup)

2 cloves garlic, minced

4 cups chicken broth, homemade if possible

2 medium new potatoes (about ¾ pound), peeled and cut into 1-inch chunks

½ pound curly kale, stems and ribs removed, finely chopped

½ teaspoon salt

1½ cups canned unsweetened pumpkin

¼ teaspoon ground nutmeg

⅛ teaspoon white pepper

¾ cup half-and-half

1 Cook the bacon over medium heat in a large Dutch oven until brown and crispy. Remove it from the pot, crumble, and set aside. Pour off all but about 1 teaspoon of the fat.

2 Heat the olive oil in the same pan and add the onion. Cook for about 5 minutes, stirring occasionally, until soft and onion starts to caramelize. Add the garlic and cook 1 minute longer.

3 Pour two cups of the broth into the pan and stir to loosen browned bits on bottom of pan. Add the potatoes, kale, and salt; bring to a boil, then reduce the heat and simmer for 20 to 25 minutes, until the potatoes are easily pierced with a fork and the kale is wilted.

4 Purèe the potato mixture with a hand-held blender or in a standing blender. There will be flecks of green from the kale. Be careful not to let hot soup splatter on you. Return the soup to the pot.

5 Stir the remaining broth and the pumpkin, nutmeg, and pepper into the soup. Taste and adjust the seasonings, if desired. Add the half-and-half and heat through, but do not boil.

6 Sprinkle each steaming bowl with the reserved bacon and serve.

Kale

Kale, with its curly leaves and dusky colors, is aesthetically pleasing. In fact, some varieties are purely ornamental, even though edible. Kale's real power is its nutritional value and fairly strong flavor, which can be tempered with other ingredients, such as pumpkin. As with many dark greens, kale is low in fat, carbohydrates, and calories. It is extremely rich in vitamins A and C and is a great source of vitamin E. It is not lacking in calcium, iron, and some B vitamins, either.

To prepare the kale, fold the leaves in half lengthwise and cut out the rib. Stack several leaves and cut crosswise into thin ribbons. Kale can be braised in a little broth and served with crumbled bacon as a side dish. Adding a little kale to your favorite soups gives quite a nutritional boost.

Tarragon **Pumpkin Soup**

A simple, velvety pumpkin soup brightened with tarragon's light anise flavor is a perfect first course for the fall table. If you can't get pumpkin, try butternut squash. For a quicker version, use canned unsweetened pumpkin.

SERVES 4

1 tablespoon olive oil

1 medium onion, chopped
(1½ cup)

2–3 pounds fresh pumpkin, seeds
and fibers removed, peeled,
and coarsely chopped (6 cups)

2 cloves garlic, peeled

1 teaspoon salt

3 cups vegetable or chicken
broth, plus more to thin
the soup, if necessary

Freshly ground black pepper

1 teaspoon dried tarragon

½ cup sour cream or nonfat
yogurt (optional)

1 Heat the oil in a large heavy-bottomed saucepan over medium heat. Add the onion and cook for 5 minutes, or until soft and lightly browned.

2 Add the pumpkin, garlic, and salt and cook for several minutes, until the pumpkin begins to brown. Pour in the broth and bring to a boil over medium-high heat. Simmer, partially covered, for 20 to 25 minutes, until the pumpkin is tender.

3 Use an immersion blender or a standing blender to purée the soup into a thick and creamy mix. If too thick, add a little more broth. Just before serving, stir in a few grinds of pepper and the tarragon. Serve with a dollop of the sour cream on each bowl of steaming soup, if desired.

Roasted Carrot-Pumpkin Soup
with Parsley Cream

Roasting brings out the natural sugars of vegetables and adds another layer of flavor to this velvety soup. Parsley cream provides a tangy counterpoint. Serve with cornbread and buttered green beans for a delightfully colorful meal.

SERVES 6

SOUP

- 2 **pounds fresh unpeeled pumpkin, seeds and fibers removed, cut into large chunks**
- 1 **pound carrots, peeled and cut into 1-inch chunks (about 2 cups)**
- 1 **tablespoon olive oil**
- ½ **teaspoon salt**
- 1 **tablespoon unsalted butter**
- ⅓ **cup minced shallots**
- 1 **tablespoon peeled and minced fresh ginger**
  Pinch of ground cloves
- 4½ **cups chicken broth**
- ⅛ **teaspoon white pepper**

PARSLEY CREAM

- ½ **cup goat cheese or fromage blanc, at room temperature**
- 3 **tablespoons finely chopped parsley**
- 2 **tablespoons heavy cream**

1 Heat the oven to 400°F.

2 Toss the pumpkin, carrots, and oil together in a large roasting pan. Bake for 45 minutes, or until the carrots and pumpkin are tender when pierced with a fork and lightly browned on the edges. Remove from the oven. When cool enough to handle, peel the pumpkin and cut into 2-inch chunks. Mash the carrots and pumpkin together and season with the salt.

3 Meanwhile, melt the butter in a large saucepan. When it bubbles, add the shallots and cook for 2 to 3 minutes over medium heat, until wilted and beginning to brown. Add the ginger and cloves while stirring. Add the broth and stir well.

4 Add the carrots and pumpkin to the pot. Purée the soup with a hand-held blender or a standing blender in batches. Return it to the pot and season with the pepper to taste. Simmer the soup, covered, for about 15 minutes.

5 While the soup is gently simmering, whisk together the cheese, parsley, and cream in a small bowl. Place a dollop of parsley cream atop each steaming bowl of soup.

Harvest Pumpkin Soup

Leeks, apples, pumpkin, and cider sing of autumn, the time to bring in the harvest and gather together around a steaming tureen of hearty, spicy soup. Feel the warmth and inhale the aromas while tasting the fruits of the land. Enjoy with a hearty loaf of whole wheat peasant bread.

SERVES 8

2–3 pounds fresh pumpkin, seeds and fibers removed, cut into chunks

1 large leek, cleaned, white part chopped

1 medium onion, chopped

½ celery root, peeled and chopped

2 large tart apples, such as Granny Smith, peeled, cored and chopped

7 cups chicken broth, homemade if possible

1 teaspoon peeled and grated fresh ginger

1 teaspoon crumbled fresh sage or ½ teaspoon dried sage

1 teaspoon dried thyme

½ teaspoon salt

¼ teaspoon ground turmeric
Dash of nutmeg
Freshly ground black pepper

1 cup apple cider

½ cup plain nonfat yogurt

1 cup grated sharp Cheddar (optional)

1 Microwave the chunks of pumpkin on high for 5 minutes or until easily pierced with a fork. When cool enough to handle, peel and coarsely chop enough to make 4 cups. Store the rest in the refrigerator for up to a week or in the freezer for up to 3 months.

2 Gently steam the leeks, onion, celery root, and apples in a large Dutch oven or soup pot with ½ cup of the stock until soft, about 10 minutes.

3 Add the remaining stock and the pumpkin. Bring to a boil, reduce heat to low, and simmer for about 10 minutes, or until the vegetables are tender. Add the ginger, sage, thyme, salt, turmeric, nutmeg, and a few grinds of pepper. Simmer for another 5 minutes. Taste and adjust the seasonings, if desired.

4 Process about half of the soup in a blender or with a hand-held blender. Return the puréed soup to the pot and stir in the cider and yogurt. It should be slightly chunky. Gently heat, but do not boil. Sprinkle each bowl of hot soup with a little Cheddar, if using.

NOTE: If you are in a hurry, try substituting one 15-ounce can of unsweetened pumpkin for the fresh pumpkin. The soup will be thicker and less chunky, but equally tasty.

Split Pea Pumpkin Soup

You might wonder what could improve this classic soup. Imagine the lush color and rich texture created by the addition of pumpkin, and you will wonder no more. Enjoy this soup on a raw winter day for a hearty lunch or light supper.

SERVES 6

1 pound dried split green peas, rinsed and picked over

1½ pounds meaty ham hock, or leftover ham bone

10 cups water

2 bay leaves

½ cup peeled and chopped celery root

1 pound fresh pumpkin, seeds and fibers removed, peeled and chopped (about 2 cups)

3 cloves garlic

1 large onion, cut in thick slices

½ teaspoon salt

½ teaspoon dried thyme

1 tablespoon canola oil

Freshly ground black pepper

1 Place the peas, ham hock, water, bay leaves, and celery root in a large Dutch oven or soup pot. Bring to a boil, partially cover, and cook for 1 hour, stirring occasionally.

2 Heat the oven to 400°F. Meanwhile, toss the pumpkin, garlic, onion, salt, and thyme with the oil in a roasting pan. Roast for 20 to 30 minutes, stirring several times, until the pumpkin is tender, and the onion lightly browned.

3 Scrape everything into the soup pot and cook covered for another 45 minutes, stirring occasionally.

4 Remove and cool the ham hock. Cut bits of meat from it and add them to the soup. Add the pepper to taste. If too thick, add a little more water and reheat.

Roasted Corn
Pumpkin Chowder

Corn chowder is a winner, and with pumpkin added you get a fabulous soup. A nice crusty loaf of bread and a salad of butter lettuce go well with this hearty favorite.

SERVES 8

1 pound fresh pumpkin, seeds and fibers removed, cut into chunks

3 cups frozen corn

4 slices bacon

1 onion, chopped (about 1 cup)

1 red bell pepper, chopped

¾ pound (about 8 small) yukon gold potatoes

5 cups chicken broth

1 teaspoon salt

½ teaspoon dried thyme

⅛–¼ teaspoon white pepper

1 cup half-and-half

1 cup grated Cheddar

1   Heat the oven to 400°F. Grease a sheet pan with oil. Rub the chunks of pumpkin with oil and bake for 35 minutes, or until slightly tender. Reduce the oven to 350°F. Add 2 cups of the corn and cook 30 minutes more, stirring occasionally, until the corn is lightly toasted and the pumpkin tender. Cool. Peel the pumpkin and cut into ½-inch cubes.

2   Meanwhile, cook the bacon in a Dutch oven until crispy. Drain, crumble, and set aside. Pour off all but 1 tablespoon of the bacon fat and cook the onion in the fat for about 5 minutes, until it is wilted. Add the bell pepper and continue cooking for 3 minutes.

3   Add the potatoes, broth, salt, thyme, and white pepper. Bring to a boil, reduce heat, and simmer, partially covered, for 15 minutes, until the potatoes are tender.

4   Add the pumpkin to the soup, along with the roasted corn and the remaining frozen corn. Continue cooking for another 10 minutes, until the pumpkin is quite soft.

5   Add the half-and-half and cook only until heated through. Don't let it boil.

6   Serve topped with the cheese and crumbled bacon.

Italian Pumpkin Soup with *Crushed Amaretti Cookies*

Judy Witts, the "Divina Cucina" sent me this recipe from Chef Fabio Picchi of the famed Cibreo Restaurant in Florence, Italy. In spring, he makes it with yellow bell peppers; in the fall, with pumpkin. Judy uses it in her cooking classes. Its straightforward flavor is made charming by the drizzle of olive oil and the small pile of Parmesan and crushed amaretti on top of each steaming bowl. You definitely want to serve this soup with a plain loaf of Tuscan bread or olive bread.

SERVES 6

1 medium yellow onion, finely chopped

1 medium carrot, finely chopped

1 stalk celery, finely chopped

1 tablespoon olive oil

1 teaspoon crumbled dried sage

½ teaspoon salt

2 pounds fresh pumpkin or butternut squash, seeds and fibers removed, peeled, cut into 1-inch chunks

3 medium Yukon gold potatoes, cut in half (about ¾ pound)

4 cups chicken broth

1 bay leaf

Fruity olive oil, for drizzling

6 tablespoons freshly grated Parmesan

6 amaretti cookies (Italian almond cookies)

1 Mix the onion, carrot, and celery together on a large cutting board and chop them some more to make what Italians call "sofritto," a mix that begins many a soup or stew.

2 Pour the olive oil into a large pot or Dutch oven and heat over medium-high heat. Add the sofritto and cook for about 5 minutes, stirring, until the vegetables begin to turn golden brown. Stir in the sage and salt.

3 Add the pumpkin, potatoes, broth, and bay leaf. Bring to a boil and cook, partially covered, for 30 to 45 minutes, until the pumpkin and potatoes are easily pierced with a fork. Remove the bay leaf and purèe in batches in a blender or with a hand-held blender until silky smooth. Add water if it seems too thick.

4 In Tuscan style, drizzle a little of the fruity olive oil on each serving, add a spoonful of Parmesan, and crush a cookie on top. Serve with a flourish.

Great American Beer Soup

This unique soup developed by Candy Schermerhorn features the intense flavors of roasted onion, reduced chicken stock, and beer all blended together with pumpkin and sour cream for smoothness and tang. Serve hot with a hearty loaf.

SERVES 6

1 medium onion, unpeeled

6 cloves garlic, unpeeled

2/3 cups pecans or walnuts

1/2 teaspoon salt

1/4 teaspoon ground allspice

1/4 teaspoon ground ginger

1 cup amber lager or any full-bodied beer that isn't extremely bitter

4 cups chicken or vegetable stock, simmered until reduced to 2 cups

1 1/2 cups canned unsweetened pumpkin

1 cup sour cream

1 egg

1/2 cup nonfat milk

Salt and freshly ground black pepper

1 Heat the oven to 350°F.

2 Roast the unpeeled onion in a roasting pan for about 1 hour, until it's softened like a baked potato and easily pierced with a fork. Roast the unpeeled garlic with the onion for the last 20 minutes; the nuts for the last 10 minutes. Cool the onion before peeling.

3 Squeeze the garlic into the bowl of a food processor and add the onion, nuts, salt, allspice, and ginger, and process until fairly smooth. Add some of the broth if needed.

4 Heat together the beer, stock, and pumpkin in a large saucepan over medium-low heat. Stir in the puréed onion mixture and simmer for 15 minutes. Remove from the heat and stir in the sour cream.

5 Beat the egg and milk together and, stirring constantly, slowly pour into the soup. Gently cook and stir for another 5 to 7 minutes until it just begins to thicken over very low heat, being careful that the soup doesn't boil. Season with the salt and pepper to taste.

Thai Pumpkin Soup

𝒯he wonderful thing about Thai curry is the heat you feel at the back of your throat while enjoying the smooth coconut, ginger, and pumpkin flavors in your mouth. This velvety soup makes a lovely light lunch with crunchy crackers, pita bread, or naan. Thai green curry paste is available in the Asian section of the supermarket, or in Asian or gourmet food stores.

SERVES 4

1 tablespoon unsalted butter

1 small onion, chopped (about 1 cup)

1 tablespoon peeled and minced fresh ginger

1 clove garlic, minced

2 cups canned unsweetened pumpkin

1½ cups coconut milk

1½ cups nonfat milk

½ teaspoon Thai green curry paste

Pinch of dried thyme

1 teaspoon freshly squeezed lime juice

½ teaspoon salt

Freshly ground black pepper

⅓ cup chopped peanuts (optional)

1 Melt the butter in a large saucepan over medium heat. Sauté the onion, ginger, and garlic in the butter until the onion is soft, about 3 minutes.

2 Place half of the pumpkin, the coconut milk, milk, curry paste, and thyme into a blender. Add the onion mixture and purée until smooth.

3 Pour the soup back in the pot, add the remaining pumpkin, and continue to cook over medium heat until it is heated through but not boiling, about 3 minutes.

4 Season with the lime juice and salt and the pepper to taste. Adjust the seasonings. Serve hot. Scatter a few chopped peanuts, if using, over each serving.

Party Menu

*T*HIS TIME OF YEAR IS A GREAT EXCUSE to have a pumpkin potluck. What follows are some great party recipes. Or you could truly rely on potluck and ask your friends to bring their favorite pumpkin recipe, hoping that you will not be deluged with pumpkin pie and pumpkin soup.

*Pumpkin Martinis

*Pumpkin Smoothies

*Mulled Pumpkin Beer

Beer and Wine

*Black Bean Dip and Chips

*Pepita Party Mix

*Pumpkin-shaped Cheeseball
and Assorted Crackers

*Blue Cheese and Pumpkin Galette

*Roasted Ginger Pumpkin–Pear Soup

Roast Turkey Breast

*Roasted Pumpkin and Barley Pilaf

Large Salad of Mixed Greens

*Pumpkin Baked Alaska with Pumpkin Ice Cream

SALADS

PUMPKIN BRIGHTENS THE COLOR palette of winter salads when tossed with dark green and purple leaves. Crunchy pepitas spark the softer greens and fruits of summer salads. The nutty sweetness of pumpkin seed oil enhances any salad. Add it to your stable of oils to sprinkle over salads along with good quality wine vinegars and balsamics.

Salads are a great way to increase the amount of vegetables we eat each day and a wonderful way to use up extra pumpkin. Add some purée to a salad dressing to add body. Scatter roasted pumpkin seeds for added flavor and crunch. Be creative.

Winter Salad
with Maple Pumpkin Dressing

SERVES 4

This salad of bitter greens sweetened with cranberries and pears and topped with nuts, tangy cheese, and a wonderfully complex dressing is a meal in itself. It also goes perfectly with creamy soups and winter stews.

MAPLE PUMPKIN DRESSING

- 2 tablespoons cider vinegar
- 2 tablespoons pure maple syrup
- 2 tablespoons soy sauce
- 1 tablespoon minced shallots
- 1 clove garlic, minced
- 1 teaspoon Dijon mustard
- ¼ teaspoon salt
- ½ cup olive oil
- ¼ cup pumpkin seed oil (see box at right)

SALAD

- 1 small head frisée, washed
- 3 cups washed baby spinach
- 1 Anjou pear, cored and cut into thin slices
- ¼ cup dried cranberries
- ¼ cup pecans, lightly toasted and chopped
- 2 tablespoons chèvre cheese

1 To make the dressing, mix the vinegar, maple syrup, soy sauce, shallots, garlic, mustard, and salt together in a small bowl. Slowly drizzle olive oil into the bowl, whisking constantly. Do the same with the pumpkin seed oil. This makes about 1 cup. Store what is left in a glass jar or bottle for several weeks in the refrigerator.

2 Break the frisée into small pieces and toss with the spinach. Arrange ¼ of the pear slices on top and scatter the cranberries and pecans over the pears. Dot with bits of chèvre and drizzle with the dressing. Toss lightly before serving.

Pumpkin Seed OIL

Pumpkin seed oil, cold pressed from the dark green hulless seeds of a pumpkin that only grows in southeastern Austria, adds a unique aroma and flavor to this salad. The seeds are gently roasted before being ground and pressed, giving the oil its signature aroma of toasted pumpkin with a nutty sweetness. Try drizzling the oil on fish, chicken, or pumpkin soup. Austrian pumpkin seed oil is available in gourmet shops or online. If you can't find it, use olive oil.

Spinach Salad
with Bacon and Pepitas

SERVES 6

A little tart, a little sweet, some crunch, some smooth — this salad has it all. Served with an omelet, this makes a lovely lunch or light supper.

2 slices bacon

1 large sweet onion, Vidalia or Walla Walla White, thinly sliced (about 2 cups)

4 cloves garlic, peeled

¼ teaspoon salt

4 tablespoons olive oil

Freshly ground black pepper

¾ pound fresh baby spinach

2 Fuji apples, or other crisp, sweet apples, washed, cored, and cut into ½-inch cubes

3 tablespoons cider vinegar

3 tablespoons apple juice

⅓ cup shelled pumpkin seeds (pepitas)

3 ounces crumbled blue cheese

1 Heat the oven to 400°F.

2 Cook the bacon in a medium skillet until crisp. Drain on paper towels, crumble and set aside. Pour out all the bacon grease and wipe out the skillet with a paper towel.

3 Mix the onion, garlic, and salt with 1 tablespoon of the oil. Roast in the oven for 25 to 30 minutes, or until the onion and garlic cloves are soft and lightly caramelized. Stir a few times while cooking. Season with a few grinds of pepper.

4 Mix the spinach and apples in a large bowl. Drizzle the vinegar and apple juice over the bowl and toss.

5 Heat the remaining 3 tablespoons of olive oil in the medium skillet over medium heat. Add the pepitas and toast for 2 to 3 minutes, until they start popping and turn light brown.

6 When the onion mixture is done, mix with the spinach and apples. Pour the hot oil and toasted pepitas over the salad and toss everything together. The spinach will wilt a bit. Scatter the bacon and blue cheese on top, add a grinding of pepper, and serve immediately.

Composed Red Cabbage and Maple Roasted Pumpkin Salad

This salad presents a rich painter's palette, with deeply purple cabbage providing the background for splashes of orange pumpkin brightened with flecks of creamy white chèvre. For color and zesty flavor, it is the perfect accompaniment to roast pork or chicken. Add crisp roasted potatoes to make a complete harvest meal.

SERVES 6

½ pound fresh pumpkin, seeds and fibers removed, cut in big chunks

   Oil for brushing pumpkin

1 tablespoon pure maple syrup

2 strips bacon

1 teaspoon olive oil

½ small head red cabbage, thinly sliced (about 4 cups)

1 tablespoon balsamic vinegar, plus more for sprinkling

¼ cup minced parsley

½ teaspoon salt

1 Granny Smith apple, cored and cut into ¼-inch dice

2 tablespoons crumbled goat cheese

2 tablespoons toasted chopped pecans

   Freshly ground black pepper

1 Heat the oven to 400°F. Brush the inside and outside of each pumpkin chunk with oil. Rub the maple syrup on the insides of each chunk. Bake for 45 minutes, or until easily pierced with a fork.

2 Cool slightly, peel, and dice. Measure out 1 cup and either store the rest in the refrigerator for up to a week, or freeze it for up to 3 months.

3 Cook the bacon until crisp in a large nonstick skillet. Pour off all but 1 teaspoon of the fat and add the oil to the skillet.

4 Cook the cabbage in the oil over medium heat until limp, about 3 minutes. Add the vinegar and stir for a few seconds. Remove from the heat and stir in the parsley and salt. Mix in the apple.

5 Set out six plates and arrange equal portions of the cabbage mixture on each plate. Scatter some pumpkin over each, and top with the cheese and the pecans. Season with the pepper to taste and an additional sprinkle of balsamic vinegar. Serve at room temperature.

Cannellini Bean
& Chicken Salad with
Pumpkin Dressing

SERVES 4

Cannellini beans and sage are an Italian classic that comforts the soul whether served hot or cold. Add chicken and a richly flavored dressing and serve this salad at room temperature for a delightful light supper.

1 whole boneless, skinless chicken breast, or 2 cups of leftover cooked chicken breast

4 teaspoons olive oil

1 can (15 ounces) cannellini beans, rinsed and drained (about 2 cups)

3/4 teaspoon crumbled dried sage leaves

1/2 teaspoon salt

Freshly ground black pepper

1/4 cup red onion, finely chopped

2 cups chopped fresh spinach

1 Heat the oven to 350°F.

2 Rub the chicken breast with 1 teaspoon of the olive oil. Cut the breast in half and place both pieces in a low baking dish in the oven for 20 to 30 minutes, or until the chicken is tender and no longer pink inside. When cool, cut into ½-inch chunks.

3 While the chicken is cooking, place pumpkin seeds in a baking pan with 1 teaspoon of the olive oil and the sea salt and roast for 3 minutes, or until the seeds start popping.

4 Heat the remaining 2 teaspoons oil in a large skillet over medium heat. Add the beans, sage, salt, and pepper to taste and cook for 5 minutes to blend the flavors. Cool, and stir in the onion.

5 Divide the spinach among 6 salad plates and spoon some of the bean mixture on top of each mound. Top with the chicken chunks.

PUMPKIN DRESSING

- 2 tablespoons unsweetened canned pumpkin
- 2 tablespoons balsamic vinegar
- ¼ teaspoon salt
- 2 tablespoons canola oil
- 2 tablespoons pumpkin seed oil (see page 49), or olive oil

GARNISH

- ½ cup roasted pumpkin seeds (pepitas)
- ¼ teaspoon sea salt

6 To make dressing, whisk together the pumpkin, vinegar, and salt. Drizzle in the oils slowly, continuing to whisk.

7 Drizzle dressing over each salad and scatter some pepitas and sprinkle a pinch of salt on top.

Mixed Greens with Purple Pepper & Orange

SERVES 4

A vision of purple, chartreuse, and orange topped with bits of white, this salad pleases many senses. Purple peppers have a crisp sharpness that is softened by the sweet of the orange and the tang of the feta. Their deeply purple outside and brilliant chartreuse inside makes a spectacular contrast in the salad. You will find them at farmers' markets and gourmet shops. In this recipe, you can be as flexible about the quantities as you wish.

1 head Romaine, cored, washed and spun dry

4 sprigs of watercress

1 purple bell pepper, cored seeded and thinly sliced

1 orange, peeled and separated into sections without the membrane

4 tablespoons feta

½ cup pumpkin seeds (pepitas)

1 teaspoon olive oil

¼ teaspoon sea salt

DRESSING

4 tablespoons balsamic vinegar

4 tablespoons good-quality olive oil

1 Place several crunchy Romaine leaves on four salad plates and cut crosswise. Lay a sprig of watercress on top.

2 Arrange equal portions of the pepper slices on each plate and top with equal portions of the orange sections. Crumble 1 tablespoon of feta on each plate.

3 Place the pepitas, oil, and sea salt in a toaster oven set at 300°F. Toast for 3 minutes, or until the pumpkin seeds pop.

4 Drizzle 1 tablespoon vinegar and then 1 tablespoon olive oil over each salad. Scatter a few pepitas over each plate and enjoy the different flavors and textures.

Roasted Potato
Pumpkin Salad

How many different potato salads have you eaten lately? This one combines tradition with innovation. Pumpkin's role is to add color and a depth of flavor to the bright combo of potatoes, bacon, parsley, red onion, celery, and tangy dressing. I love warm, freshly made potato salad, and that is how I recommend serving this. I always marinate the hot potatoes in vinegar. For this recipe, I have found that Russet potatoes take up the sharp taste better than the waxy new potatoes I use in other potato salads.

SERVES 6

1   tablespoon olive oil

1½   pounds Russet potatoes, peeled and cut into 1-inch chunks

½   pound fresh pumpkin, seeds and fibers removed, peeled, cut into ½-inch chunks

2   tablespoons cider vinegar
     Freshly ground black pepper

3   slices bacon

3   tablespoons mayonnaise

2   tablespoons sour cream

1   teaspoon sea salt

½   teaspoon dry mustard

¼   teaspoon sugar

¼   cup finely chopped celery root, or 2 tablespoons chopped celery

¼   cup red onion, chopped

¼   cup minced parsley

1   Heat the oven to 400°F.

2   Spread the oil on a jelly-roll pan. Spread the potatoes and pumpkin on the pan and roll them around to coat with the oil. Roast in the oven for 30 minutes, or until easily pierced with a fork.

3   While still hot, place the potatoes and pumpkin chunks in a medium bowl and sprinkle with 1 tablespoon of the vinegar and a few grinds of pepper. Let sit for 20 minutes.

4   Meanwhile, cook the bacon until browned and crispy. Drain on paper towels, crumble, and set aside.

5   Mix together the mayonnaise, sour cream, the remaining vinegar, salt, mustard, and sugar in a small bowl and pour over the warm potatoes. Sprinkle the celery root, onion, parsley, and bacon over the salad and gently stir until everything is mixed together. Serve warm, or at room temperature.

Autumn Toasted
Couscous Salad

Israeli couscous, a larger version of Moroccan couscous, is the size of peppercorns, has a nutty flavor, and is ideal for salads. Toasting the couscous deepens its flavor and enhances this savory and colorful mix of pumpkin, fennel, and cranberries, brightened with specks of parsley.

SERVES 6

- 1½ pounds fresh pumpkin, seeds and fibers removed, cut into chunks
- 1 tablespoon olive oil
- 8 ounces Israeli couscous (about 1¼ cups)
- 1½ cup apple juice
- ½ teaspoon sea salt, plus more to taste
- ½ cup fresh parsley, finely minced
- ⅓ cup dried cranberries, chopped
- ⅓ cup fennel root, finely chopped
- ¼ cup red onion, minced
- 2 tablespoons grapeseed oil, or substitute olive oil
- 2 tablespoons red wine vinegar
- Freshly ground black pepper

1 Microwave the chunks of pumpkin on high for 5 minutes, or until almost tender.

2 When cool enough to handle, peel, and coarsely chop enough to make 2 cups. Store the remainder in the refrigerator for up to a week or in the freezer for up to 3 months.

3 Heat the olive oil in a large skillet over medium heat. Add the couscous and cook for 2 to 3 minutes, until the couscous browns a bit. Add the apple juice, reduce the heat, and simmer, covered, for 15 to 20 minutes, until the liquid is absorbed and the couscous is almost tender, stirring occasionally. Add the pumpkin and cook 1 to 2 minutes longer, stirring to blend the flavors and color.

4 Transfer the couscous to a large bowl, sprinkle with the salt, and cool slightly. Toss with the parsley, cranberries, fennel, and onion. Stir in the grapeseed oil and vinegar. Season with a few grinds of pepper. Taste and add more salt, if desired. Serve at room temperature.

Grapeseed OIL

Grapeseed oil, a mild oil with a slightly nutty flavor, is a product of wine country. After pressing the grapes for the production of wine, the seeds are extracted from the pomace, which is left over after the juice is squeezed from the grapes. The seeds are dried, pressed, and bottled. This is a frugal way to use the leftovers, and the product is amazing. Grapeseed oil can be substituted for olive oil in salads, sauces, and cooking. Its high smoke point makes it popular for high-heat cooking. And, to top it off, grapeseed oil is high in antioxidants and very low in saturated fats. I love to use it in salad dressings. It is available from the Napa Valley Grapeseed Oil Company or at gourmet grocery stores.

Spring Spinach and Strawberry Salad
with Pepitas

This sprightly salad is my springtime favorite with its tasty mix of flavors and textures, fresh crisp spinach leaves, sweet strawberries, creamy avocado, crunchy pepitas, and tangy cheese. It can accommodate other seasonal ingredients, but these are the ones I like best. For a more formal presentation, compose this salad in the same way on individual plates, and serve as a separate course.

SERVES 4

- ½ pound washed and dried baby spinach
- 1 pint fresh strawberries, hulled and cut in half, or in quarters, if very large
- 1 avocado, peeled and cut into ½-inch chunks
- ¼ purple onion, peeled and thinly sliced
- 3 tablespoons crumbled blue cheese
- ¼ cup pumpkin seeds (pepitas)
- 3 tablespoons olive or grapeseed oil
- 2–3 tablespoons balsamic vinegar
- Freshly ground black pepper

1 Place the spinach in a large salad bowl. Arrange the strawberries on top. Scatter the avocado, onion, and cheese over the strawberries.

2 Place the pepitas on the tray of a toaster oven set at 300°F. Toast for 2 to 3 minutes, or until they pop.

3 Drizzle with the oil and vinegar, and top with a few grinds of pepper. Toss the salad as you serve it.

TIP: I always wash spinach and lettuce, even if it comes in a package that says it is washed. Spin it and dry it. Wrap it in paper towels, place all in a plastic bag, and store in the refrigerator until ready to use. If farmers' markets are available to you, substitute a mix of fresh tender greens for the spinach.

SIDE DISHES

Pumpkin as a vegetable all by itself can be roasted, grilled, steamed, puréed, and mashed. Butter, salt, pepper, and herbs bring out pumpkin's luscious flavor. It can enhance many a side dish with its bright color and a mild flavor that rarely overwhelms.

The recipes that follow are only a beginning to the many ways that savory pumpkin can stand alone or enhance other ingredients. Cooks in Mexico, Italy, Africa, and Asia regularly use pumpkin. It is indeed a super food.

Grilled Pumpkin

Here is a very simple way to prepare pumpkin when you are grilling chicken, pork, or beef. Add some rosemary, sage, or thyme to the oil and pumpkin mix for added flavor.

SERVES 6

1½ pounds fresh pumpkin, seeds and fibers removed, peeled, cut into 1-inch wedges (about 3 cups)

2 tablespoons olive oil

1 tablespoon balsamic vinegar

1 teaspoon dried oregano

½ teaspoon salt

Freshly ground black pepper

1 Heat the grill to high. Yes, that was quite intentional.

2 Toss the pumpkin chunks with the oil, vinegar, oregano, salt and a few grinds of pepper. Spread the pumpkin on the grill, reduce the heat to medium, and cook the pumpkin wedges about 5 minutes on each side, or until easily pierced with a fork.

Grated Candied Pumpkin

Here is another quick and simple way to create a sweet and spicy pumpkin side dish. Serve with salmon or chicken.

4 SERVINGS

1 tablespoon butter

1 pound fresh pumpkin, seeds and fibers removed, peeled, and grated (about 3 cups)

½ teaspoon salt

⅛ teaspoon ground cumin

2 tablespoons pure maple syrup

Freshly ground black pepper

¼ cup chicken broth

1 Heat the butter in a medium skillet over medium heat for 1 minute. Add the pumpkin, salt, and cumin and cook, stirring, for about 5 minutes, until the pumpkin wilts.

2 Add the syrup and pepper to taste and continue cooking and stirring for 1 minute longer. Add the broth and cook until it mostly evaporates, about 2 minutes. Serve hot.

Golden Roasted Vegetables

his is a beautiful mix of fall root vegetables. If peeling all those roots is too depressing a thought, parboil the pumpkin, rutabaga, and beets until the skins come off easily. Roast for a shorter period of time. It is worth the effort to do all that peeling to get the roasted blend of flavors. Serve with roast poultry or pork.

SERVES 6

1 pound fresh pumpkin, seeds and fibers removed, peeled, cut into 2- by 1-inch wedges

1 pound golden beets, peeled and cut into 2- by 1-inch wedges

1 rutabaga, peeled and cut into 2- by 1-inch wedges

1 pound carrots, peeled and cut in half if very thick, and into 2-inch lengths

4 large shallots, peeled, trimmed, and cut in half lengthwise

4 cloves garlic, smashed and peeled

2 teaspoons kosher salt

Freshly ground black pepper

2 tablespoons olive oil

1 tablespoon minced fresh herbs, such as rosemary, thyme, and sage (optional)

1 Heat the oven to 400°F.

2 Toss the pumpkin, beets, rutabaga, carrots, shallots, garlic, salt, pepper to taste, and oil together in a large bowl. Place in a large roasting pan and roast, stirring occasionally, for 45 minutes, or until the vegetables are caramelized and tender when pierced with a fork.

3 Scatter herbs over roasted vegetables.

NOTE: Kosher salt is flakier and therefore less dense that table salt. I like its clean, less salty flavor. You may find yourself using more to get the saltiness you desire.

Mashed
Potatoes and Pumpkin

This rich, rustic mix with a light orange hue will not turn away the potato purists, and it will satisfy your soul as much as any pile of mashed potatoes does. Light-skinned cheese pumpkins with a lovely thick, pale flesh, are larger than sugar pumpkins and wonderful in this mash. If available, try them; if not, use a sugar pumpkin. If you prefer a version that is lower in fat, use half-and-half or milk instead of heavy cream.

SERVES 6

4 unpeeled Yukon gold potatoes, scrubbed and cut into eighths

¼ Long Island cheese pumpkin, seeds and fibers removed, peeled, cut into 2-inch chunks (about 2 cups)

½ cup heavy cream

1 tablespoon butter

1 teaspoon salt

1 Place the potatoes and pumpkin chunks in a large saucepan covered with salted cold water. Bring to a boil over medium-high heat, cover, reduce the heat to medium-low, and cook for 15 to 20 minutes, until the potatoes and pumpkin are very tender when pierced with a fork. Drain.

2 Return the potatoes and pumpkin to the saucepan and mash them with a potato masher over very low heat to thoroughly dry them out, being careful not to scorch them.

3 Add the cream to the pot and let it warm up, about 1 minute. Once the cream is warm, continue mashing, to mix in the cream.

4 Stir in the butter and salt and serve while hot.

Pumpkin Purée
with Almond Topping

staff staple of our Thanksgiving table, this sweetened and enriched pumpkin is one of the many harvest dishes affectionately dubbed "yucky" vegetables by family and friends, who demand them each year.

SERVES 8

2 pounds fresh pumpkin, seeds and fibers removed, cut into chunks

¼ cup plain nonfat yogurt

3 tablespoons brown sugar

1 tablespoon butter, softened

1 egg, slightly beaten

½ teaspoon salt

¼ teaspoon nutmeg

¼ cup chopped toasted almonds, (reserve 1 tablespoon for topping)

1 Cook the fresh pumpkin in a microwave on high for 5 minutes, or until easily pierced with a fork. When cool enough to handle, peel, measure 4 cups, and mash.

2 Heat the oven to 350°F. Grease a 2-quart casserole with butter.

3 Mix together the pumpkin, yogurt, brown sugar, butter, egg, salt, nutmeg, and almonds thoroughly, but not excessively. Pour into the prepared casserole.

4 Sprinkle the reserved almonds over top and bake for 30 to 40 minutes, until bubbly.

TIP: To toast the almonds, spread them on the tray of a toaster oven. Set the temperature to 350°F and toast for 5 to 10 minutes, until fragrant and lightly browned.

Spinach *and* Pumpkin

Most of the pumpkins used in African cooking are more like the Latin American calabaza, lighter, longer, and larger than sugar pumpkins. Jessica Harris shared this Kenyan recipe from The African Cookbook: Tastes of a Continent, *Simon & Schuster, 1998. This simple combination is a colorful blend of distinctive flavors and a great way to use leftover roasted pumpkin. Instead of spinach, try this recipe with fresh tomatoes and a pinch of sugar. Add it to a vegetarian table, or serve with meat, poultry, or fish. This recipe is easily doubled for a crowd.*

SERVES 4

- 1 **tablespoon peanut oil**
- 1 **medium onion, thinly sliced (about 1½ cups)**
- 1 **package (10 ounces) frozen spinach, cooked and drained, or 1 pound of fresh spinach, cooked and chopped (about 1½ cups)**
- 1½ **cups roasted pumpkin (see pages 8–9), mashed**
- ½ **teaspoon salt**

1 Heat the oil over medium heat in a large skillet. Cook the onion in the oil for 5 to 7 minutes, or until soft and lightly browned.

2 Stir in the spinach, pumpkin, and salt. Cook over low heat, without stirring, for 5 to 7 minutes, or until a brown crust forms on the bottom. Serve hot.

Cape Malay Pumpkin

Jessica Harris, in her book The African Cookbook: Tastes of a Continent, *describes this South African dish as similar to candied sweet potatoes (see also page 64). Sugar and spice with a surprise of apricot makes this pumpkin casserole a sweet treat to accompany poultry or pork.*

SERVES 4

- 1 pound fresh pumpkin, seeds and fibers removed, peeled, cut into ¾-inch chunks
- ¼ pound fresh apricots, pitted and chopped, or 2 ounces dried apricots, minced
- ½ cup freshly squeezed orange juice
- 1 teaspoon brown sugar
- ½ teaspoon ground cinnamon
- 1 tablespoon unsalted butter

1 Heat the oven to 350°F. Spray the inside of a 1½-quart ovenproof dish with cooking spray.

2 Place the pumpkin, apricot, and orange juice in the dish. Stir to mix. Sprinkle with the sugar and cinnamon and dot with the butter.

3 Cover and bake for 30 minutes, or until the pumpkin is easily pierced with a fork and a little mushy. Serve hot.

Wild Mushroom
Pumpkin Risotto

Risotto always requires your attention, and this is no exception. To add layers of flavor means adding more steps. In this case, it is worth every stir of the spoon to get the earthy, mushroom flavor along with the sweetness of the caramelized pumpkin permeating every grain of rice. Risotto is wonderful with any kind of grilled meat, poultry, or fish, or as a light meal by itself.

SERVES 6

1 pound fresh pumpkin, seeds and fibers removed, cut into big chunks

Oil for brushing on pumpkin

¾ ounce dried Porcini mushrooms, or mixed dried mushrooms

3–4 cups chicken broth

2 tablespoons butter

½ cup finely diced onion

2 cups arborio rice

¼ teaspoon salt

1 cup white wine

¼ cup grated Parmesan

1 Heat the oven to 400°F. Brush each chunk of pumpkin with the oil. Bake for 45 minutes, or until the pumpkin is easily pierced with a fork.

2 When cool enough to handle, dice and measure out 1½ cups of pumpkin. Store the rest in the refrigerator for up to a week or freeze it for up to 3 months.

3 Cover the mushrooms with hot water and let them sit for about 20 minutes. Drain through a fine sieve; reserve the water, and set the mushrooms aside.

4 Add enough of the chicken broth to the reserved mushroom water to make 4 cups and heat in a medium saucepan over medium heat.

5 Melt one tablespoon of the butter in a large heavy-bottomed saucepan over medium heat and cook the onion in the butter for several minutes until wilted. Add the rice and salt and cook until rice is translucent and glistens with butter. Add the pumpkin and wine to the pan, reduce the heat to medium-low, and continue to cook until the wine evaporates, about 2 minutes.

6 Ladle about one cup of the remaining broth into the pot and stir frequently as the rice absorbs the liquid. While the mixture is still moist, add more broth and continue to stir. Repeat until the broth is gone. (The final ladle should include cooked mushrooms; see step 7.)

7 While the rice is cooking, cook the prepared mushrooms over medium heat in the remaining tablespoon of butter for several minutes until they release their liquid. Stir into risotto with the final ladle of broth.

8 Remove the pot from the heat, stir in the cheese, cover the pot, and let it sit for 2 minutes to finish the absorption. Serve while hot. After all the work, be sure to savor every mouthful.

Sage-Pumpkin *Risotto*

Some have called making risotto an act of love. True, it takes time, attention, and care to produce this deceptively simple dish of the Piedmonte in Northern Italy. Pumpkin adds a subtle twist and pale orange tone to this traditional version.

SERVES 4

3 cups chicken broth, homemade if possible

1 tablespoon butter

3 fresh sage leaves

1 tablespoon olive oil

1 cup arborio rice

2 tablespoons minced shallots

½ pound fresh pumpkin, seeds and fibers removed, peeled, grated (about 1 cup)

½ cup white wine

1 teaspoon salt

Freshly ground black pepper

Pinch of saffron

¼ cup grated Parmesan

1 Heat the broth in a medium saucepan over medium heat. Simmer while making risotto.

2 Melt the butter over medium-low heat in a large, heavy-bottomed saucepan. Add the sage leaves and fry for a minute or two, until crisp.

3 Add the oil to the saucepan and heat over medium heat for 1 minute. Add the rice and shallots and cook, stirring, for about 2 minutes, until the rice becomes slightly translucent and glistens. Add the pumpkin, wine, salt, and pepper to taste and cook until the wine evaporates, about 3 minutes.

4 Ladle about one cup of the hot broth into the pot and stir frequently as the rice absorbs the liquid. Continue this process of adding a ladle of broth, stirring and cooking until the broth is gone, mixing the saffron in with the last bit of broth. This will take 18 to 20 minutes.

5 Add the sage and the cheese, cover the pot, and let sit for 2 minutes. Serve immediately.

Apple, Cranberry, and Pumpkin Stuffing

ENOUGH TO STUFF A 16-POUND TURKEY *or* TO SERVE 12 AS A CASSEROLE

Fill the bird with apples, cranberries, onion, celery, pumpkin, bread crumbs, sage, and thyme, and let the juices seep through with this aromatic mix, or cook in a casserole. Either way, this is deeply satisfying.

1 pound fresh pumpkin, seeds and fibers removed, cut into big chunks

Oil for brushing pumpkin

1 package (16 ounces) stuffing mix

2 Granny Smith, or other tart apples, cored and chopped (about 2 cups)

2 stalks celery, chopped (about 1 cup)

1 large onion, chopped (about 1½ cups)

1 cup fresh cranberries

1 tablespoon crumbled dried sage

2 teaspoons salt

1 teaspoon dried thyme

Freshly ground black pepper

1 tablespoon unsalted butter

2½ cups boiling water

1 Heat the oven to 400°F. Brush the pumpkin chunks with oil. Bake for 45 minutes, or until the pumpkin is easily pierced with a fork.

2 When the pumpkin is cool enough to handle, mash slightly and measure 2 cups. Store the rest in the refrigerator for up to a week or freeze it for up to 3 months.

3 Reduce the oven to 350°F. Grease a 2-quart casserole dish with butter, if preparing as a side. (You may need to do this even if you're stuffing a bird, to cook the extra.)

4 Thoroughly combine the pumpkin, stuffing mix, apples, celery, onion, cranberries, sage, salt, thyme, and pepper to taste in a large bowl. Use your hands to distribute the seasonings and vegetables among the crumbs.

5 Melt the butter in the boiling water and add to the dry mix. Thoroughly mix with your hands until the crumbs are moistened.

6 Spoon the stuffing into the prepared casserole dish and bake for 45 minutes. Alternatively, stuff a rinsed and dried 16-pound turkey and put the overflow in a small casserole dish. Roast the turkey according to your usual method, or follow a recipe.

Roasted Pumpkin and
Barley Pilaf

Almost any grain lends itself to pilaf, but I love the nuttiness of barley in this version, which enhances any buffet table. The recipe was inspired by one in A Private Collection *by the Junior League of Palo Alto, California. It is a wonderful make-ahead dish that is easily doubled for a crowd. It goes well with just about everything.*

SERVES 6

1 pound fresh pumpkin, seeds and fibers removed, cut into big chunks

Oil for brushing pumpkin

2 tablespoons unsalted butter

½ cup chopped shallots

1 cup pearl barley

½ teaspoon crumbled dried sage, or 1 tablespoon fresh minced sage

1 teaspoon salt

Freshly ground black pepper

4 cups chicken broth, homemade if possible

½ cup chopped fresh parsley

⅓ cup pine nuts, lightly toasted

1 Heat the oven to 400°F. Brush the pumpkin chunks with oil. Bake for 45 minutes, or until the pumpkin is easily pierced with a fork.

2 When cool enough to handle, cut the pumpkin into ¼-inch cubes and measure 1 cup. Store the rest in the refrigerator for up to a week or freeze for up to 3 months.

3 Reduce the oven to 350°F. Grease a 2-quart casserole dish with butter.

4 Melt the butter in a large skillet over medium-high heat. Reduce the heat to meduim, add the shallots, and cook for 5 minutes, until they begin to caramelize. Add the barley and continue cooking for several minutes. Season with the sage and salt and cook 1 minute longer.

5 Add the pumpkin and a few gratings of pepper, and mix well. Transfer the mixture to the casserole dish. Warm up the broth in a saucepan, then add to the casserole, along with the parsley and pine nuts.

6 Bake for 1 hour, stirring once, or until the barley has absorbed the broth and is tender.

Roasted Pumpkin Parmesan Polenta

Different cultures create versions of the same dishes in their cuisines. Examples of this are polenta, a staple of Italian cooks; cornmeal mush in New England; and South African "Isijingi," which is corn porridge with pumpkin and maybe a little peanut butter. Serve this with grilled sausages and a crisp salad or with chicken, pork chops, or steak accompanied with steamed vegetables.

SERVES 6

1 pound fresh pumpkin, seeds and fibers removed, cut into big chunks

Oil for brushing the pumpkin

1 teaspoon crumbled dried sage

2 tablespoons minced shallots

1 tablespoon olive oil

4 cups chicken broth

1 cup dry polenta

½ teaspoon salt

1 tablespoon butter

½ cup freshly grated Parmesan

1 Heat the oven to 400°F. Brush each pumpkin chunk with oil and place in a roasting pan. Bake for 45 minutes, or until the pumpkin is easily pierced with a fork.

2 When cool enough to handle, roughly mash enough to measure 2 cups, scraping up the brown parts. Store the rest in the refrigerator for up to a week or freeze it for up to 3 months.

3 Return the mashed pumpkin to the roasting pan and add the sage and shallots. Drizzle with the olive oil and roast for another 10 to 15 minutes, until the shallots soften.

4 Heat the chicken broth in a large saucepan over medium-high heat until it boils. Reduce the heat to low, and gradually add the polenta in a thin stream, stirring constantly. Add the salt and continue to cook over low heat, stirring occasionally, until the mixture thickens, about 20 minutes.

5 Stir in the pumpkin mixture and then the butter and cheese. Cook and stir for a few minutes, until just combined.

Golden Pumpkin
Corn Pudding

Call me old-fashioned, but creamy corn pudding, holding plump sweet kernels of corn and fragrant with thyme, is the perfect complement to any meal of roasted or grilled chicken, turkey, or pork and steamed broccoli or green beans. It can be made ahead and baked before serving, and is best served warm, not hot.

SERVES 4

2 tablespoons unsalted butter

1 cup chopped onion

3 cups frozen corn kernels or fresh kernels cut from the cob

1 tablespoon sugar

1 teaspoon salt

Freshly ground black pepper

¼–½ teaspoon dried thyme

2 tablespoons unbleached all-purpose flour

2 eggs

1¼ cups nonfat milk

½ cup canned unsweetened pumpkin

1 Heat the oven to 325°F. Butter a 1½-quart casserole dish.

2 Melt the butter in a large skillet over medium heat. Cook the onion in the butter for 3 minutes, or until softened. Turn off the heat and add the corn, sugar, salt, pepper, and thyme. Stir to blend flavors. Sprinkle with the flour.

3 Whisk together the eggs, milk, and pumpkin in a large bowl. Scrape the corn mixture out of the skillet and mix everything together.

4 Pour into the prepared casserole dish and bake for 1 hour 15 minutes, or until the center is set and the edges lightly browned.

Thanksgiving

THANKSGIVING, the feast celebrating the gathering of the harvest, lets us give thanks. It is my favorite holiday and meal, in part because I imagine families and groups throughout the country, of all religious traditions, coming together over basically the same meal of turkey, mashed potatoes, root vegetables, and pumpkin pie often accented with their own ethnic specialties. In the good old American spirit of volunteerism, people serve this meal in shelters, senior centers, and food kitchens to those who wouldn't otherwise have it. In addition to family, people invite strangers or friends of friends to this meal. The big food-filled, welcoming table of my dreams, surrounded by people of all ages and colors, speaks to the best of our values.

Try an assortment of these turkey-friendly recipes at your Thanksgiving table.

Holiday Pumpkin Dip

Pumpkin-Shaped Cheeseball

Herbed Parmesan Twists

Pumpkin-Filled Ravioli with Fried Sage

Golden Roasted Vegetables

Mashed Potatoes and Pumpkin

Pumpkin Puree with Almond Topping

Apple, Cranberry, and Pumpkin Stuffing

Golden Pumpkin Corn Pudding

Pumpkin Gratin with Caramelized Onions

Traditional Pumpkin Pie

Southern Pecan Pumpkin Pie

Meringue Pumpkin Pie

Spicy Pumpkin Ice Cream Pie with Gingersnap Pecan Crust

Pumpkin Roll with Mascarpone Filling and Caramel Sauce

Lemon-Pumpkin Strudel

Pumpkin Gratin
with Caramelized Onions

Gratins speak of comfort, with their layers of thinly sliced vegetables, creamy cheeses, and crunchy topping. Pumpkin not only adds color and nutrition, but a wonderful subtle tang. This dish makes a terrific accompaniment to roasted or grilled chicken, turkey, pork, or beef. Complete the meal with roasted green beans.

SERVES 6

2 pounds fresh pumpkin, seeds and fibers removed, peeled, cut into 1/16-inch slices, (about 4 cups)

1/2 teaspoon salt

Freshly ground black pepper

1 tablespoon oil

1 tablespoon butter

2 medium onions, sliced

3 ounces pancetta, cut into 1/4-inch dice

1/4 teaspoon dried thyme

4 ounces Gruyère cheese, grated (about 1 1/2 cups)

1/8 teaspoon ground nutmeg

1 cup half-and-half

1 cup fresh, whole wheat bread crumbs

1 Heat the oven to 375°F.

2 Steam or microwave the pumpkin until it is just tender, about 5 minutes in a steamer, or 2 minutes in a microwave. Sprinkle with 1/4 teaspoon of the salt and pepper to taste, and set aside.

3 Heat the oil and butter in a large skillet over medium-high heat. Add the onions and pancetta and cook for 2 to 3 minutes, until soft. Season with the thyme, the remaining salt, and more pepper to taste. Reduce the heat to medium and continue cooking, stirring occasionally, until the onions wilt and begin to brown and caramelize and the pancetta becomes crisp, about 5 to 10 minutes.

4 Grease a low-sided, one-quart gratin or casserole dish with butter. Arrange half the pumpkin slices in overlapping rows in the dish. Spread the onions and pancetta evenly over the pumpkin. Sprinkle with 1 1/4 cup of the cheese and top with another layer of pumpkin slices.

5 Stir the nutmeg into the half-and-half and pour over the vegetables.

6 Mix the remaining cheese with the breadcrumbs and sprinkle over the top. Bake for 35 to 45 minutes, or until the pumpkin is easily pierced with a fork and the top is lightly browned and bubbly around the edges. Serve hot.

◆ ◆ ◆

Variation

For an equally delicious variation, try this gratin with blue cheese instead of Gruyère.

◆ ◆ ◆

HOW TO PREPARE *Breadcrumbs*

I keep the ends of whole wheat bread loaves in my freezer. When breadcrumbs are needed, I thaw them, tear them in quarters, and toss through the small hole in the top of a blender, quickly covering the hole with my hand. This is an important point, as the crumbs go flying out the top otherwise. Any excess crumbs can be stored in the freezer for later use.

Kadu
(Afghani Sweet Pumpkin)

Pumpkin simmered a sweet tomato lamb sauce, topped with yogurt and a pinch of mint, creates a wonderful layering of flavors, colors, and textures to produce this exquisite staple from the cuisine of Afghanistan. To make a heartier main course, double the amount of lamb. Use less lamb and serve the dish as an appetizer. It goes well with basmati rice, naan, or pita bread for a hearty lunch or light supper.

SERVES 6

PUMPKIN

2½ pounds fresh pumpkin, seeds and fibers removed, cut into ½-inch-wide, long slices

MEAT SAUCE

1 pound ground lamb

½ teaspoon salt

1 clove garlic, minced

2 teaspoons freshly ground or crushed coriander seeds

1 teaspoon fresh ginger, peeled and minced

1 cup plain tomato sauce

6 tablespoons sugar

YOGURT SAUCE

1 cup plain nonfat yogurt

2 cloves garlic, minced

¼ teaspoon salt

GARNISH

Dried mint leaves

1 Microwave the pumpkin on high for 5 minutes, or until easily pierced with a fork. Peel when cool enough to handle.

2 To make the meat sauce, cook the meat in a large skillet over medium heat until all the red is gone, about 5 minutes. Sprinkle with the salt. Add the garlic, coriander, and ginger, and cook for another 2 minutes. Add the tomato sauce and sugar, and simmer for 5 minutes to blend the flavors. Add the prepared pumpkin and continue simmering for another 5 minutes, until the pumpkin warms in the sauce.

3 Meanwhile, combine all the ingredients for the yogurt sauce.

4 To serve, place several slices of pumpkin on each plate, spoon some sauce over them, and top with a dollop of the yogurt sauce. Sprinkle with the mint before serving.

Cabbage Braised *in Pumpkin Ale*

This is definitely a fall dish because, unless you make your own, you will only find pumpkin ale in the fall. However, it is worth looking for some when cabbages are at their freshest to create this savory accompaniment to grilled sausages or pork chops and boiled potatoes.

SERVES 6

¼ pound pancetta, cut into ¼-inch dice, about ¾ cup

1 tablespoon corn oil

2 leeks, white part thinly sliced

1 onion, thinly sliced

1 cup pumpkin ale

1 medium head cabbage, cored and very thinly sliced

¾–1 cup chicken broth

¼ cup cider vinegar

1 teaspoon sugar

½ teaspoon salt

Freshly ground black pepper

¼ teaspoon celery seed

½ cup toasted breadcrumbs (optional) (see page 75)

1 Lightly brown the pancetta in a Dutch oven or large sauté pan over medium heat for about five minutes. Dribble the oil into a pan and, after it heats slightly, add the leeks and onion. Continue to cook, stirring occasionally, until the leeks and onion wilt, about 5 minutes.

2 Add the ale and scrape up the browned bits in the skillet. Add the cabbage, broth, vinegar, sugar, salt, a few grinds of pepper, and celery seeds.

3 Bring the mixture to a boil, cover, and simmer over low heat for about 20 minutes, or until the cabbage is soft and the liquid has almost completely cooked away. Taste, adjust the seasonings, and serve.

4 To make a casserole, heat the oven to 350°F, place the cabbage in a 2-quart casserole dish, sprinkle the crumbs on top, and bake for 15 to 20 minutes, or until the top is lightly browned.

Halloween Party
for Grown~Ups

*P*UMPKIN IS ONE FOOD that it is okay to play with. Not only does pumpkin inspire the cook, but pumpkins become the means for all forms of artistic expression. From the humble jack-o'-lantern to intricate masks created by clever carvers, pumpkins are the raw material that gets the fun started. Kids love Halloween because they can dress up, scare people, and get candy for it. Grown-ups love the chance to be kids again. Well, some do.

When planning your Halloween party for adult friends, start with a pumpkin theme on the invitation. In the fall, there is no problem in finding pumpkin paraphernalia. Try a school supply store for little pumpkin shaped pads and write your invitations on them. Have lots of pumpkins around, pumpkins of all sizes and shapes. Stack them outside and arrange them inside.

Set up a place near the kitchen for those who want to carve a jack-o'-lantern. For these carvers choose a variety of templates, carving kits, and knives. A dremel rotary tool is useful, as is a wood carving kit if you want to get sophisticated. A simple inexpensive plastic carving kit, consisting of an all-purpose saw, a detail saw, a scooper, a poker, and a drill, is available at many stores in October. Use the all-purpose saw for cutting the initial hole in the top or bottom. Scoop out the seeds. Draw a scary face on paper or use a purchased template. With the poker, push through the paper to transfer the design to the pumpkin. Use the drill for poking round holes, and the saws for carving the rest. These kits look flimsy, but they are fantastic.

OUTSIDE DECOR

Find some dried cornstalks to lean by the front door. They're a perfect background for a pile of pumpkins. Light the walkway with jack-o'-lantern, real or artificial.

TABLE DECORATIONS

Find a length of black fabric that will cover your table and a smaller textured piece of orange fabric for a runner. Make the decorations simple by strewing bittersweet down the center of the table on the runner and tucking little pumpkins, persimmons, and real or artificial autumn leaves between the branches. Hollow out some of the little pumpkins to make candlestick holders and place them randomly in the mix.

Main COURSES

*H*ere we have the heart of the savories that showcase the versatility of this wonderful gourd. Pumpkin is a natural ingredient in winter stews. It enhances pork and lamb, brightens chicken, and adds depth to vegetarian dishes. I urge you to experiment and add pumpkin to your favorite recipes. You will not be disappointed.

Blue Cheese and Pumpkin Galette

Pumpkin seasoned with sage melds into a blue cheese topping in this savory tart. Cut in small slices and serve warm or at room temperature as an appetizer. The crust needs to be refrigerated, so make it several hours ahead.

SERVES 6

1½ pounds fresh pumpkin, seeds and fibers removed, cut into chunks

1 tablespoon plus 1 teaspoon unsalted butter

½ cup minced shallots (1 large shallot)

1 teaspoon crumbled dried sage

1 teaspoon salt

Freshly ground black pepper

½ cup walnuts, finely chopped

¼ cup breadcrumbs

1 recipe Rich Pastry Dough (page 81)

1 cup crumbled blue cheese (3–4 ounces)

1 egg white

2 tablespoons grated Parmesan

1 Heat the oven to 400°F.

2 Place the pumpkin chunks in a microwave-safe dish and cook on high for 5 minutes, or until easily pierced with a fork. When cool enough to handle, peel, cut into 1- by 2-inch strips, and measure 2 cups. Store the remaining pumpkin in the refrigerator for up to a week or in the freezer for up to 3 months.

3 Melt 1 tablespoon of the butter in a large skillet over medium heat. Cook the shallots in the butter for about 2 minutes. Add the pumpkin, season with the sage, salt, and pepper to taste, and stir for about 1 minute.

4 In a medium skillet, melt the remaining 1 teaspoon butter over medium heat. Stir in the walnuts and breadcrumbs and cook for about 2 minutes, until the crumbs and nuts begin to brown.

5 Roll the dough into a 15-inch circle. Line a baking sheet with parchment paper and carefully lift the dough circle to the paper. Sprinkle the nut/crumb mixture in the center of the crust, leaving an edge of about 2 inches. Pour the pumpkin mixture over the crumbs, and scatter the blue cheese on top.

Rich Pastry Dough

DOUGH FOR 1 GALETTE

This rich dough is easy to use and very forgiving.

1 cup unbleached all-purpose flour

1 teaspoon sugar

¼ teaspoon salt

6 tablespoons unsalted butter, cut into small pieces

2 tablespoons vegetable shortening

¼ – ⅓ cup ice water

1 Stir the flour, sugar, and salt together in a medium bowl.

2 Drop the butter into the flour, toss to coat, and work it into the flour with a pastry blender or two knives until the pieces resemble tiny peas.

3 Add the shortening and continue cutting into the flour mixture until the texture is like breadcrumbs, with some pea-sized pieces.

4 Add the water bit by bit, mixing it in with a fork. Don't overmix. The dough should be moist enough to stick together when pressed.

5 Place the dough on a floured surface and, with the heel of your hand, smear it across the board in several directions. Shape the dough into a ball, wrap it in plastic, and chill in the refrigerator for several hours. The dough can be kept in the refrigerator for up to 2 days, or stored (in a freezer bag) in the freezer for up to 1 month.

6 Fold the edges of the dough over the filling. Brush the dough with egg white and sprinkle with the Parmesan.

7 Bake for 30 minutes, or until the crust is nicely browned. Cool briefly on a rack, then slide the galette onto a large serving plate before cutting into slices.

Pumpkin Pizza
with Gorgonzola

The recipe for this pizza crust was given to me years ago by a charismatic young music teacher. Since then I have taught hundreds of junior high students to make quick and easy Battistelli pizza dough, in honor of Mike the music teacher. Roll it thin for a delightfully fresh, crisp foundation. Pumpkin adds a new twist to the old tradition. For equally great results, use a fresh sugar pumpkin or a large white cheese pumpkin.

**MAKES TWO
14-INCH PIZZAS**
(Serves 6)

CRUST

1 cup warm water

1 tablespoon active dry yeast

2½ cups unbleached all-purpose flour

1 tablespoon canola oil

1 teaspoon salt

1 teaspoon sugar

1 To make the crust, combine the water and yeast in a medium bowl and let them sit until the yeast is dissolved, about 1 minute. Whisk in 1 cup of the flour, the oil, salt, and sugar. Continue whisking until mixture is smooth.

2 With a wooden spoon, stir in another cup of the flour, until flour is thoroughly incorporated.

3 Spread the remaining ½ cup of flour on a large board and scrape the dough onto the board. Sprinkle some of the flour on top of the dough. Knead the dough at least 10 times, until it is soft, smooth, and no longer sticky. Cut it in half, cover with a clean towel, and let it rest for 10 minutes. This literally allows the dough to relax, making it easier to roll out. You will be amazed at how thin you can roll out this dough if it is well rested.

4 Heat the oven to 450°F.

5 While the dough is resting, toss together the fresh pumpkin, shallots, 1 tablespoon of the sugar, oil, sage,

4 cups fresh sugar or cheese pumpkin, seeds and fibers removed, peeled

⅓ cup minced shallots

3 tablespoons brown sugar

2 tablespoons olive oil

2 teaspoons dried, crumbled sage

1 teaspoon salt

Freshly ground black pepper

1 cup canned unsweetened pumpkin

2 tablespoons cornmeal

1 cup crumbled gorgonzola cheese

salt, and pepper to taste in a roasting pan. Roast for 15 minutes, stirring occasionally, until the pumpkin is easily pierced with a fork. Slightly mash the pumpkin and set aside.

6 Raise the oven temperature to 475°F.

7 Mix the canned pumpkin with the remaining 2 tablespoons brown sugar.

8 To assemble the pizza, roll out half the dough into a 14-inch circle. Dust a baking sheet with 1 tablespoon of the cornmeal and lift dough onto the sheet. Crimp the edge to make a small lip. Spread half the canned pumpkin mixture over the top and scatter half the roasted pumpkin on it. Dot with half the gorgonzola and cook for 10 minutes, or until the crust is slightly browned and the cheeses are melted.

9 Repeat with the other piece of dough.

Family PIZZA NIGHT

Sunday night is pizza night at our house. All family members are invited and, since our family is small, we never have more than 12 at the table. I love pizza. It is one of my favorite foods. Making a crust from scratch is not that hard, and the result is so satisfying that I like to keep a batch in my freezer. Bottled tomato sauces are great, though I usually use a very simple canned tomato sauce. Pumpkin pizza is a fun variation in autumn and a great activity for kids. Teens can take on the whole job. Preschoolers love to spread and scatter.

If I am making more than two pizzas, I make multiple batches of dough, roll out each, placing them on cookie sheets in the freezer until ready to assemble and bake. Leftover dough can be frozen in a lump, thawed, and rolled out later. It will keep in the freezer for up to two months.

Pumpkin-Filled Ravioli
with Fried Sage

Italians love their Zucca and, in this classic dish, use pumpkin or butternut squash. Judy Witts, a wonderful cooking teacher who lives in Tuscany, tipped me off to adding Mostarda di Cremona, which adds a sweet mustardy layer of flavor. This recipe uses packaged wonton skins for the pasta, which saves time in this labor-intensive dish. But if you always make your own pasta, go for it. Amaretti are airy, crunchy Italian almond cookies that easily crumble. Look for the real thing. Serve with a salad of mesclun, arugula, walnuts, and gorgonzola; steamed broccoli; and a loaf of Italian ciabatta.

SERVES 6 *as a main dish,* **12–15** *as appetizers*

- 6 tablespoons unsalted butter
- ½ cup finely chopped shallots
- 24 whole fresh sage leaves , plus 1 tablespoon minced
- ¼ teaspoon salt

  Freshly ground black pepper
- 1¼ cup canned unsweetened pumpkin
- ¾ cup freshly grated Parmesan
- ¼ cup crushed amaretti cookies
- 2 tablespoons dried breadcrumbs
- 2 tablespoons minced Mostarda di Cremona (optional)
- ¼ teaspoon ground nutmeg
- 24 wonton skins or wraps (1 package)

1 Melt 2 tablespoons of the butter in a large skillet over medium heat. Cook the shallots in the butter for 2 minutes. Season with the 1 tablespoon minced sage and the salt and pepper to taste, and cook for 1 minute. Stir in the pumpkin and cook over medium heat until it loses some of its moisture and the mixture thickens, about 3 minutes.

2 Stir in ½ cup of the cheese; the cookies; bread crumbs; the Mostarda, if using; and nutmeg. Set aside.

3 To assemble the ravioli, lay out the wonton squares on a smooth, clean surface. Place 1 tablespoon of the filling in the center of each square. Using your finger, moisten around the edges of a ravioli square with cold water. Place a second square over the first one and press firmly around all edges to make a perfect seal. Also press out any air bubbles that have formed. Repeat with the rest of the squares and cover loosely with plastic wrap until ready to cook.

4 Rinse out the skillet and melt the remaining 4 tablespoons butter over medium heat. Add the sage leaves and cook until they shrink, darken slightly, and become crispy. The butter will brown.

5 To cook the ravioli, bring a large pot of salted water to a boil. Drop half the ravioli in at a time. Cook until they rise to the top of pot, 2 to 3 minutes. With a slotted spoon, gently scoop out the cooked ravioli and place in a colander. Repeat with the second half.

6 For each serving, place 4 ravioli on a plate, drizzle with the brown butter and fried sage leaves, and sprinkle with the remaining Parmesan.

NOTE: These can be made in the morning and covered tightly with plastic wrap and stored in the refrigerator. If kept much longer, the filling may seep into the dough. The prepared ravioli may also be frozen for up to a month. Place them on a cookie sheet and quickly freeze them. Store in a freezer bag in the freezer and thaw slightly before cooking.

MOSTARDA *di Cremona*

These particular Italian sweet fruit pickles packed in a mustard syrup are a specialty that dates back to the days of the Roman Empire from city of Cremona. Other cities have their own mostarda mix. Use these pickles with poultry, grilled meats and sausages, as well as with mild cheeses. You will find them in Italian markets. Mostarda di Cremona is a lovely addition to the ravioli, but optional because it can be hard to find.

Cheddar-Pumpkin Tart

MAKES ONE 9-INCH TART
(Serves 8 as a side dish, 6 as a main dish, and 16 as hors d'oeuvres)

This lovely tart can accompany a salad and grilled chicken for a nice summer meal, or it can be the meal. Cut it in small pieces or make it in small muffin cups to serve as hors d'oeuvres. However you do it, enjoy the blend of sharp Cheddar with mild pumpkin in this savory tart.

1 **fully baked Savory Tart Crust (page 87)**

2 **teaspoons butter**

1 **teaspoon canola oil**

1 **medium onion, thinly sliced (about 1½ cups)**

½ **teaspoon salt**

¾ **cup canned unsweetened pumpkin**

2 **eggs**

½ **cup half-and-half**

½ **teaspoon dried thyme**

⅛ **teaspoon ground white pepper**

3½ **ounces sharp Cheddar, grated (1½ cups)**

1 Heat the oven to 375°F.

2 Melt 1 teaspoon of the butter with the oil in a large skillet over medium heat. Cook the onion in the skillet for 10 to 12 minutes, stirring frequently, until soft and beginning to brown. Sprinkle with ¼ teaspoon of the salt and set aside.

3 Beat the pumpkin and eggs together in a medium bowl. Add the half-and-half, the remaining ¼ teaspoon salt, thyme, and pepper to taste.

4 To assemble the tart, scatter the cooked onion on the bottom of the cooled crust. Sprinkle the cheese over the onion. Pour the pumpkin mixture on top and spread it over the cheese. Dot with the remaining teaspoon of butter and bake for 30 to 40 minutes, or until a knife inserted in the center comes out clean. Serve hot, warm, or at room temperature.

Savory Tart Crust

**DOUGH FOR ONE
9-INCH TART CRUST**

1 cup unbleached all-purpose
flour

½ cup whole wheat pastry flour

¼ cup grated fresh Parmesan

½ teaspoon salt

8 tablespoons (1 stick) cold
unsalted butter, cut into
small pieces

1 egg yolk

¼ cup cold water

1 Use a 9-inch fluted tart pan with a removeable bottom for this recipe. Do not substitute another pan.

2 Mix the flours, Parmesan, and salt together in the bowl of a food processor. Add the butter and pulse until the mixture looks like coarse crumbs. Dump the mixture into a large bowl.

3 Beat the egg yolk and water together and mix into the crumbs. When combined, form the dough into a ball and place on the counter. Flatten into a disk and, with the heel of your hand, smear the dough toward the edge about 6 times. Flatten into a disk, wrap in plastic wrap, and refrigerate for several hours.

4 To roll out the dough, place the flattened disk between 2 sheets of waxed paper. Roll the dough slightly bigger than the 9-inch tart pan. Place it in the pan and trim any excessive overhang to ½-inch. Fold the outer edge into the tart pan to make a double edge. Refrigerate the dough for 30 minutes before baking.

5 To fully bake the crust, heat the oven to 400°F.

6 Line the dough with aluminum foil. Fill with dried beans or pie weights. Bake for 10 minutes. Remove the foil and weights, prick the bottom and sides of the dough with a fork, and bake 10 minutes longer, or until the crust is golden brown. If the crust has risen up, carefully poke it with a fork to release the air. Cool on a wire rack and proceed with the recipe.

Crêpes with Spinach and Creamy Pumpkin Sauce

Chicken crêpes were a family favorite when my kids were growing up. I often had a stack of crêpes and some chicken in the freezer and could quickly put them together. This dressed-up version with or without chicken can be made ahead and baked just before serving time. The pale orange béchamel sauce has great aesthetic appeal, not to mention the subtle pumpkin flavor. Wraps could substitute for crêpes, though they are not as light and delicate as the real thing. Try this with a crisp Waldorf salad of apples, nuts, red onions, and celery, or, for less crunch, toss butter lettuce with sliced red onions and grated cucumber.

SERVES 4

CRÊPES

- ¾ cup nonfat milk
- 2 eggs
- ½ cup flour
- ½ teaspoon salt
- 2 tablespoons unsalted butter for cooking crêpes

SAUCE

- 2 tablespoons butter
- 2 tablespoons unbleached all-purpose flour
- 2 cups milk
- ⅓ cup canned unsweetened pumpkin
- ½ teaspoon salt
- ¼ teaspoon ground nutmeg

1 To make the crêpes, place the milk and eggs in a blender and whirl until well blended. Add the flour and salt, and mix until thoroughly combined. The batter can be stored in the refrigerator for several hours while you prepare the sauce and filling.

2 To cook crêpes, use an 8-inch skillet. Melt ¼ teaspoon of the butter in the skillet over medium-high heat. Pour ¼ cup of the batter into the skillet and quickly grab the handle of the pan and circle it around to spread the batter over the entire bottom of the skillet. Cook the crêpe for less than 1 minute, until the batter becomes dull on top and looks cooked through. With a spatula, lift it out of the skillet and place it on a plate.

3 Repeat this procedure until the batter is gone and you have a stack of 8 crêpes. Extra crêpes can be double wrapped in plastic wrap and frozen for up to 4 weeks.

FILLING

- 1 **tablespoon butter**
- ½ **medium onion, chopped (about ½ cup)**
- 1 **pound fresh spinach, washed, steamed, drained and chopped (about 1½ cups), or 1½ 10-ounce packages frozen chopped spinach, thawed and drained**
- 6 **ounces Swiss cheese, grated (about 2 cups)**
- 2 **cups cooked chicken breast halves (optional), cut into ½-inch pieces**

4 To make the sauce, heat the butter in a medium saucepan over medium heat. Add the flour and cook over medium heat for 1 minute as the mixture bubbles. Add the milk and continue cooking for several minutes, until the mixture begins to boil and thicken. Boil for 1 minute; the mixture will be smooth and creamy. Stir in the pumpkin, salt, and nutmeg and set aside.

5 To make the filling, heat the butter in a small skillet over medium heat. Cook the onion in the butter for 2 minutes, until soft. Combine with the spinach, cheese, chicken, if desired, and 1 cup of the sauce.

6 Heat the oven to 350°F. Grease a 1-quart baking pan with butter.

7 To assemble the crêpes, lay out 8 crêpes on a clean surface. Divide the filling equally among them and roll them up. Place the crêpes seam-side down in the prepared baking pan. Cover with the remaining sauce and bake for 20 to 25 minutes, or until bubbly.

Chicken-Pumpkin
Tacos

Each taco, overflowing with spicy vegetables and cheese, is a meal in itself. It is fun to expand the recipe and serve it to a crowd, allowing each person to build his or her own.

MAKES 6 TACOS

TACOS

- 1 tablespoon canola oil
- 1 onion, thinly sliced
- 1½ pounds boneless, skinless chicken breast halves
- 2 red peppers, seeded and chopped
- 1 pound fresh pumpkin, seeds and fibers removed, peeled and diced (about 2 cups)
- ¼ cup canned unsweetened pumpkin
- ½ cup canned tomatoes and juice
- 2 teaspoons chili powder
- 1 teaspoon ground cumin
- Dash of hot sauce
- 1 teaspoon salt

- 1 tablespoon freshly squeezed lime juice
- 1 tablespoon minced cilantro
- 6 flour tortillas, 8 inches each, or crisp corn taco shells

TOPPINGS

- ½ cup plain nonfat yogurt
- ¼ cup sour cream
- 1½ cups grated Cheddar or Monterey Jack
- 1 ripe avocado, peeled and chopped
- 3 cups shredded lettuce
- 1½ cups salsa

1 Heat the oil in a large skillet or sauté pan over medium-high heat. Add the onion and cook for 3 minutes, or until wilted. Add the chicken and peppers and cook for another 3 minutes. Stir in the fresh and canned pumpkin, tomatoes, chili powder, cumin, hot sauce, and salt. Cover, reduce the heat, and simmer until the chicken is tender and no longer pink, the pumpkin is easily pierced with a fork, and the sauce thickens, about 10 to 15 minutes. When the chicken is cool enough to handle, shred it and return it to the pan. Stir in the lime juice and cilantro and let the mixture sit while you heat the tacos.

2 On a griddle or large skillet, over medium heat, warm the tortillas for 1 minute on each side. Place one on each of 6 plates and divide the filling among them. Combine the yogurt and sour cream in a small bowl. Top each taco with the yogurt mix, cheese, avocado, lettuce, and salsa.

3 Fold in half as you eat them.

Pasta with Pumpkin
and Wild Mushrooms

This smoky, creamy blend of flavors and textures is a great way to use up leftover grilled chicken. To grill the chicken, rub it with olive oil, and grill over medium-low heat for 30 minutes, or until cooked through. Turn regularly so the surface doesn't burn. Serve with a sourdough baguette and a salad of field greens.

SERVES 6

2 cups (2 ounces) dried porcini or other dried mushrooms

1 tablespoon olive oil

1½ pounds fresh sugar or cheese pumpkin, seeds and fibers removed, peeled, cut into ½-inch cubes (about 3 cups)

1 tablespoon finely chopped fresh sage

1 teaspoon salt, plus more to taste

1 large clove garlic, minced

3 skinless, boneless chicken thighs, grilled (about ¾ pounds) (optional)

¾ cup heavy cream

½ cup freshly grated Parmesan, plus additional for serving

Freshly ground black pepper

12 ounces fusilli or other spiral pasta

1 Place the mushrooms in a small bowl with 2 cups of hot water. Let sit for 20 minutes, then drain and chop the mushrooms, reserving the liquid.

2 Heat the oil in a large skillet or sauté pan over medium heat. Add the pumpkin, sage, and ½ teaspoon of the salt, and cook, stirring frequently, for 5 minutes, or until the pumpkin is slightly tender. Add the garlic, ½ cup of the mushroom liquid, and the mushrooms. Stir for another minute to scrape up the brown bits.

3 If using grilled chicken, cut into 1-inch pieces and add to the skillet. Cook for several minutes over medium-low heat to blend the flavors. Add another ½ to ¾ cup of the mushroom liquid, the remaining salt, the cream, and the cheese. Cover and cook for several minutes over low heat, stirring occasionally, until the cheese melts into the liquid. Season with the pepper to taste. Add more salt, if desired.

4 Meanwhile, cook the pasta until al dente. Drain and serve immediately with more Parmesan.

White Bean, Chicken, and Pumpkin Chili

SERVES 8

This is a quick and easy white chili spiked with cilantro that craves a crusty loaf and a bright salad.

- 1 tablespoon olive oil
- 1 large onion, chopped (about 2 cups)
- 4 cloves garlic, minced
- ¼ teaspoon white pepper
- 1½ pounds boneless, skinless chicken breast halves, cut into 1-inch cubes
- 1–2 teaspoon salt
- 1½ pounds fresh pumpkin, seeds and fibers removed
- 1 can (15 ounces) chicken broth
- 5–6 cups (three 20-ounce cans) cannellini beans, rinsed and drained
- 1 can (4 ounces) chopped mild green chiles
- 2–3 teaspoons ground cumin
- 1–2 teaspoons green Tabasco sauce
- ¼ cup minced cilantro

1 Heat the olive oil in a Dutch oven over medium heat. Cook the onion for 1 minute. Add the garlic and pepper, and cook 1 minute longer. Add the chicken and salt, and cook for 10 minutes, stirring occasionally.

2 Microwave the pumpkin on high for 3 minutes. When cool enough to handle, peel and cut into ½-inch chunks to measure 3 cups. Store any remaining pumpkin in the refrigerator for up to a week or in the freezer for up to 3 months.

3 Stir in the broth, beans, pumpkin, chiles, cumin, and Tabasco sauce; and cook for 15 minutes over low heat, until the chicken is done and the pumpkin is easily pierced with a fork. Taste and adjust the seasonings.

4 Serve while hot, topping each serving with a pinch of the cilantro.

Moroccan Chicken & Pumpkin Stew

Tender chunks of chicken simmered with pumpkins, garbanzo beans, tomatoes, and the spices of Morocco will draw you to the aromas and flavors of this hearty stew. Serve it with crispy pumpkin seeds and steamed couscous for a perfect meal.

SERVES 6

- 1 tablespoon canola oil
- 6 boneless, skinless chicken breast halves
- 1 large onion, thinly sliced (about 2 cups)
- 3 cloves garlic, minced
- 1 teaspoon ground cumin
- 1 teaspoon coriander seeds, crushed
- 1½ pounds fresh pumpkin, seeds and fibers removed, peeled, cut into ½-inch cubes (about 3 cups)
- 2 cups chicken stock, homemade if possible
- 1½ teaspoons salt

- ¼ teaspoon turmeric
- 1 cinnamon stick
- ⅛ teaspoon cayenne
- 6 whole cloves
- Freshly ground black pepper
- 1 can (14.5 ounces) garbanzo beans, rinsed and drained
- 1 can (14.5 ounces) whole tomatoes with juice
- 2 tablespoons canned unsweetened pumpkin or leftover pumpkin purée
- 2 cups uncooked couscous
- ¼ cup roasted shelled pumpkin seeds (pepitas), for garnish

1 Heat the oil in a large Dutch oven over medium heat. Brown the chicken, about 2 minutes on each side, and remove it from the pot. Add the onion to the pot and cook, stirring, for 3 to 5 minutes, until softened. Add the garlic, cumin, and coriander seeds and cook for 1 minute longer.

2 Return the chicken to the pot along with the fresh pumpkin, chicken stock, salt, turmeric, cinnamon stick, cayenne, cloves, and a few grinds of pepper. Increase the heat and bring to a boil. Reduce the heat, cover, and simmer for 30 minutes, or until the chicken is tender and no longer pink and the pumpkin is tender.

3 Add the garbanzo beans, tomatoes, and canned pumpkin and cook for 10 minutes longer to blend flavors.

4 During this final stage, bring 2 cups of salted water to a boil. Add the couscous to the water. Cover, remove from the heat, and let sit it for 5 minutes. Fluff the couscous with a fork.

5 Serve the stew over the couscous in large soup bowls. Garnish with the pepitas.

To ROAST THE PEPITAS, combine them with 1 teaspoon oil and ¼ teaspoon salt. Roast in a toaster oven at 300°F for 3 minutes, until they start popping. (See page 11.)

Chicken in Pueblan Green Pumpkin Seed Sauce
(Pipián de Pollo)

Pumpkin seeds are featured in this classic sauce from Puebla, Mexico, which can also be made with almonds and sesame seeds. Calvin Trillin spoke glowingly about discovering this sauce on a trip to Puebla with his granddaughter. Leftover sauce is great over grilled salmon, poultry, or pork or as an enchilada sauce.

SERVES 4

- 4 chicken breast halves, with bones and skin
- 1 large white onion, sliced (about 2 cups)
- 4 cloves garlic, coarsely chopped
- 1 large carrot, peeled and thinly sliced
- 1½ teaspoons salt, plus more to taste
- 2 bay leaves
- ¼ teaspoon dried thyme

- 1 cup shelled pumpkin seeds (pepitas)
- 12 large sprigs cilantro, roughly chopped, plus several for garnish
- 2 cups small romaine leaves, roughly chopped
- 2 small jalapeño chiles, or 3 serrano chiles, seeded, ribs removed and roughly chopped
- 1 tablespoon canola oil

1 Place the chicken, half the onion, half the garlic, the carrot, 1 teaspoon of the salt, bay leaves, and the thyme in a large pot or Dutch oven with 8 cups of water. Bring to a boil over medium-high heat and skim off the foam as it rises. Partially cover, reduce the heat, and simmer for 10 to 15 minutes.

2 Remove the chicken from the broth and set it aside. Strain the broth, discarding the solids. Lay a paper towel on top of the broth to soak up the rising fat. Set the broth aside. Meanwhile, remove skin and bones from chicken and tear the meat into large chunks.

3 To make the sauce, toast the pepitas in a large skillet over medium heat until they have popped and turned golden, about 5 minutes. Spread them on a plate to cool, reserving a few for garnish.

4 Combine the cooled seeds with the remaining onion, the remaining garlic, the cilantro, romaine, and chiles in a blender. Add 1½ cups of the broth and blend until smooth.

5 Heat the oil in a large saucepan over medium heat. Add the purée and stir constantly until very thick, about 10 minutes. Stir in 2 more cups of the broth, partially cover, and simmer over medium-low heat for 10 minutes. The sauce will look coarse. Taste and adjust the seasonings.

6 Add chicken to the sauce and cook it over low heat to warm the chicken in the sauce. Don't let the sauce boil. With a slotted spoon, remove the chicken and place it on a serving platter. Spoon the sauce over it, and garnish with the reserved sprigs of cilantro and pumpkin seeds.

NOTES:
- Freeze the extra broth for use in soups and stews.
- Store the extra sauce in the refrigerator for up to a week to use in other dishes.
- This dish can be made ahead.
- Store the chicken and sauce separately in the refrigerator. Gently reheat them before serving.
- For more people, add a few more pieces of chicken to the poaching pot.
- For a quicker and easier meal, poach the chicken in 6 cups of canned chicken broth and proceed from step 3.

Roast Chicken
with Harvest Vegetables

Roast chicken is what I cook when I want something easy and wonderful. It always pleases. There must be thousands of methods to roast this basic bird, and I was always on a quest for the best. With this recipe, I stopped looking. This is a great one-pan meal with herb-flavored crispy skin, soft savory vegetables, and moist, tender chicken. If you have the time, I highly recommend brining the chicken before cooking for a deliciously moist result. To do this, rinse the chicken and place it in a large kettle. Add ½ cup kosher salt and ¼ cup sugar. Cover with cold water and ice cubes. Let sit for an hour, several if you have time. Remember to add more ice.

SERVES 4

1 roasting chicken, 5–6 pounds, at room temperature or brined

4 cloves garlic

1 tablespoon plus 1 teaspoon fresh rosemary, minced

1 tablespoon fresh sage leaves, minced

2 teaspoons kosher salt, plus additional for rubbing into skin

2 teaspoons fresh thyme leaves, or ½ teaspoon dried

2 tablespoons unsalted butter, softened

Freshly ground black pepper

1 small rutabaga or yellow turnip (¾ pound), peeled and cut into 2- by 1-inch wedges (2–3 cups)

2 small Russet potatoes, peeled and cut into quarters lengthwise (about 2 cups)

2 medium onions, peeled and cut into quarters from top to bottom (about 2 cups)

1 teaspoon olive oil

1 pound fresh pumpkin, seeds and fibers removed, peeled, cut into 2- by 1-inch wedges (about 2 cups)

1 Heat the oven to 450°F.

2 Rinse and pat the chicken dry with paper towels.

3 Place the garlic, 1 tablespoon of the rosemary, the sage, 1 teaspoon of the salt, and the thyme on a cutting board. Using a large chef's knife, mince them all together with the butter.

4 Gently lift the skin from the breast of the chicken and the drumsticks. Smear the herb butter under the skin. Sprinkle additional salt and some pepper over the skin. Place the chicken on a V-shaped rack in a large, 11- by 16-inch roasting pan.

5 Toss the rutabaga, potatoes, and onions with the remaining rosemary, the remaining salt, and the oil in a large bowl. Strew the rutabagas, potatoes, and onion around the chicken in the roasting pan.

6 Place the pan in the lower part of the oven and roast for 20 minutes. Remove from the oven and add the pumpkin to the vegetables. Stir to mix the vegetables with the juices.

7 Reduce the oven to 350°F and return the pan to the oven. Continue roasting for 1 to 1½ hours, or until the internal temperature of the chicken reaches 170°F and the vegetables are tender. The chicken will no longer be pink inside, the juices will run clear, and the drumsticks will move easily.

8 Remove the pan from the oven. Lift the chicken onto a serving platter and cover with aluminum foil. Stir the vegetables in the pan so they are covered with the juice and, with a slotted spoon, remove them to a serving dish. Taste and add salt and pepper if desired. Cover the dish with foil. Turn off the oven and place the chicken and vegetables in the cooling oven while making the sauce.

9 Place the roasting pan on the stovetop. Remove most of the grease by floating a paper towel on top of the pan. Do this several times, until all that remains is the juice and a little fat. Turn the heat to medium and cook and stir until the juices begin to caramelize.

10 Slice the chicken, arrange on the platter, pour the pan juices over it and serve with the vegetables.

Barbecued Chicken Thighs
with Spicy Pumpkin Sauce

This dark sweet-and-sour sauce, enriched by pumpkin, glazes the chicken as it sizzles on the grill, leaving a crispy, crunchy coating over the succulent and tender chicken. If you prefer to use boneless, skinless chicken thighs, reduce the cooking by a few minutes.

SERVES 4

8 chicken thighs

BARBECUE SAUCE
MAKES 2 CUPS

¾ cup cider vinegar

¼ cup orange juice

½ teaspoon hot sauce

¼ cup Dijon mustard

⅓ cup dark brown sugar

2 tablespoons Worcestershire sauce

2 tablespoons molasses

½ cup canned unsweetened pumpkin

1 Rinse the chicken in cold water and pat dry with paper towels. Set in low, flat dish. Turn the grill to high.

2 Whisk all the sauce ingredients together in a small bowl. Brush both sides of the chicken with the sauce, cover the dish with plastic wrap, and let sit at room temperature for 30 minutes. Bring remaining sauce to a boil, reduce heat to low, and simmer for five minutes.

3 Reduce the grill to medium-low and place the chicken thighs on it. Cover the grill and cook for a total of 20 to 30 minutes, or until the chicken is tender and no longer pink. Brush with more sauce and turn every 5 to 10 minutes to avoid flare-ups and charring. Reduce the heat to low or scatter the coals if you notice charring.

NOTE: The trick to barbecuing chicken is to cook it thoroughly and yet keep it juicy without flaming the skin or surface. This is not something to throw on the grill, sit down with a beer, and watch the clock for a half hour. It requires tending and adjusting and poking. If the meat is really squishy, it is not done. If it is hard, too bad: You blew it, the chicken is overdone. When poked, the chicken should feel firm with a little give.

Boil the leftover sauce for at least five minutes and it will keep for up to a month in a covered jar in the refrigerator. Use for other chicken barbecues or grilled pork.

Celebrate the Harvest

*F*ALL IS FLEETING, BEAUTIFUL, AND PRECIOUS if you live in a cold climate and know what lies ahead. Scrunching through a carpet of red, yellow, and orange leaves, smelling the scent of dried leaves wafting in the air; and enjoying the slanted afternoon sunlight brightening the hillsides is the essence of autumn. Instead of light summer salads and tender vegetables, hearty stews and steaming soups get our juices flowing. The harvest is in and the markets are filled with pumpkin, winter squash, and root vegetables. What better way to say good-bye to the waning summer sun than to invite your friends for an early fall celebration of the harvest?

* Ginger Roasted Pear Soup

* Pumpkin-Filled Ravioli
with Fried Sage

*Pork Tenderloin
with Red Wine Sauce

Pumpkin Sauce

* Pumpkin Gratin
with Carmelized Onions

Steamed Brussels Sprouts

* Pumpkin Roll with Mascarpone
Filling and Caramel Sauce

TABLE DECORATIONS

For a tablecloth, use a length of orange fabric, or fabric that is predominately orange to cover the table. Cover the bottom of a wide, low glass vase with chestnuts to a depth of several inches; scatter some bittersweet berries over the top. Add a variety of mums including chartreuse Fuji mums into the chestnuts to make a low, loose arrangement. Fill the vase with water and place it on a rectangle of mirror glass in the center of the table. Use orange, brown, or deep orange candles and brown napkins. For fun place-card holders, make a vertical slit in little munchkin pumpkins alongside the stem. Write the names of guests on pieces of brown cardstock and insert one in each slit. Place a pumpkin place card at each table setting.

On a sideboard fill a large wooden bowl, preferably rectangular, with cleaned and polished root vegetables and colorful peppers.

Mexican Pumpkin Lasagna

Layers of beans, cheese, peppers, and salsa tucked between tortillas makes this Mexican lasagna a crowd pleaser for all ages and a great dish to bring to a potluck. Pumpkin is a subtle addition, adding color, texture, and a boost of vitamins to this healthful dish.

SERVES 10

1 tablespoon canola oil

¾ pound ground turkey

1 medium onion, chopped (about 1½ cups)

1 can (14.5 ounces) whole tomatoes

1 tablespoon chili powder

2 teaspoons ground cumin

½ teaspoon salt

Freshly ground black pepper

2–3 drops hot sauce

1 cup kidney beans, rinsed, drained, and mashed

¾ cup canned unsweetened pumpkin

½ red bell pepper, seeded, and chopped into ¼-inch dice (about ½ cup)

½ green bell pepper, seeded, and chopped into ¼-inch dice (about ½ cup)

1–2 jalapeño chiles, seeded, and minced

8 flour tortillas, 8 inches each

1½ cups light sour cream

6 ounces sharp Cheddar, grated (about 1½ cups)

6 ounces Monterey Jack, grated, (1½ cups)

1 cup mild or medium salsa

¼ cup chopped fresh cilantro

TIP: For a large crowd, double this recipe or cut it into small squares and serve it as hors d'oeuvres. If you have leftover chicken, mix it with the salsa and add it to the second layer.

1 Heat the oil in a large skillet over medium heat. Add the turkey and cook until it loses its color, about 5 minutes. Add the onion and continue cooking another 5 minutes longer, until softened. Add the tomatoes and juice, chili powder, cumin, salt, pepper to taste, and hot sauce. Mash the tomatoes slightly and cook 5 minutes longer, until the mixture is well blended and some of the liquid has cooked off.

2 Stir in the beans and pumpkin and set aside. Mix the red pepper, green pepper, and chiles together in a small bowl.

3 Heat the oven to 350°F. Grease a 9- by 13-inch baking pan with butter.

4 To assemble, lay four tortillas on the bottom of the prepared baking pan in an overlapping fashion and so they come up on the sides of the pan. Spread half the turkey mixture on top of the tortillas. Top with half the sour cream and sprinkle with 1 cup of the Cheddar and half the pepper.

5 Cover with two more tortillas and spread the remaining turkey mixture on them. Top with the remaining sour cream, 1 cup of the Monterey Jack and sprinkle with the remaining pepper.

6 Top with the remaining two tortillas. Fold the side edges over the top, spoon salsa over the tortillas, and sprinkle the remaining cheeses on top. Bake for 35 to 45 minutes, or until the top begins to turn golden and the cheese melts. Sprinkle with the cilantro, cut into squares, and serve.

Pumpkin-Turkey Medley

This dish is adapted from Martha Storey's sensationally simple recipe for putting together the last bits of Thanksgiving turkey with mashed pumpkin. For a total meal, serve this sage-seasoned comfort food with steamed or roasted green beans and whole berry cranberry sauce, or a simple tossed salad.

SERVES 6

1½ pound sugar pumpkin, seeds and fibers removed, cut into chunks (or 2 cups mashed, cooked pumpkin)

Olive oil, for rubbing on the pumpkin

2 cups bread cubes

1 tablespoon butter

1 medium onion, thinly sliced

1 teaspoon crumbled dried sage

½ teaspoon salt

Freshly ground black pepper

1 cup chicken broth

2–3 cups cooked turkey, cut into 1-inch chunks

½ cup grated sharp Cheddar

♦ ♦ ♦

Variation

This casserole works equally well with chicken or any winter squash.

♦ ♦ ♦

1 Heat the oven to 400°F.

2 Thoroughly wash the outside of the pumpkin. Rub lightly with olive oil and roast for 45 minutes, or until easily pierced with a fork. Cool slightly, then peel off the outer skin and coarsely mash enough to make 2 cups. While the pumpkin is roasting, spread the bread cubes on a cookie sheet and toast in the oven for 5 to 10 minutes, or until lightly browned.

3 Reduce the oven temperature to 350°F. Grease a 2-quart casserole dish with butter.

4 Melt the butter in a large skillet over medium-high heat. Cook the onion in bubbling butter for 5 to 7 minutes, until soft and lightly browned. Stir in the croutons, sage, salt, and pepper to taste and cook for 1 minute. Mix in the broth, pumpkin, and turkey and transfer to the prepared casserole dish.

5 Bake for 20 minutes. Sprinkle the Cheddar on top and return to the oven for another 5 to 10 minutes, or until the cheese is melted and the casserole is bubbly. Serve steaming hot.

Grilled Salmon
with Pepita Crust

Simple, but elegant, this dish is perfect with pumpkin risotto and steamed or roasted fresh beets. It's also delicious served with slices of pickled ginger from an Asian market or sushi shop.

SERVES 4

1½ pounds salmon fillet

1 tablespoon hoisin sauce

1 tablespoon olive oil

¼ teaspoon sea salt

   Freshly ground black pepper

⅓ cup shelled pumpkin seeds (pepitas)

1 teaspoon dark sesame oil

1 teaspoon ground cumin

½ teaspoon salt

   Dash of cayenne

1 Rinse and pat the salmon dry. Cut it crosswise into 2 pieces and rub both sides with the hoisin sauce and olive oil. Season with the sea salt and a few grinds of pepper. Heat the grill to high. Place the salmon skin-side down on the grill and cook for 2 minutes. Reduce the heat to medium, turn the salmon, and cook 5 to 7 minutes longer, or until the salmon is barely cooked through.

2 While the salmon is cooking, toss the pepitas with the sesame oil, cumin, salt, and, cayenne, and place them on a toaster oven tray. Toast for 3 minutes, or until the seeds pop.

3 Crush the seeds or pepitas in a mortar and pestle, or coarsely chop.

4 When the salmon is done, remove the skin and cut each piece in half to make 4 servings. Place each piece on a dinner plate, press the crushed pepitas into the top of the salmon, and scatter a few on the side.

Creamy Shrimp and Rice

Plump shrimp nestled in a gingery, coconut-infused stew of peppers, pumpkin, and rice can be made even more spectacular when brought to the table in a pumpkin shell. This dish is inspired by a recipe in Joanna Farrow's beautiful book Pumpkin. Accompany the stew with crusty bread and simple salad of greens and vinaigrette. For a variation, cook the rice separately and serve the stew on top of it.

SERVES 6

1 tablespoon canola oil

½ cup finely chopped shallots

2 large cloves garlic, minced

2 teaspoons peeled and minced fresh ginger

½ teaspoon cumin seeds

1 cup brown basmati rice

1 pound fresh pumpkin, seeds and fibers removed, cut into chunks

1 medium red bell pepper, seeded and cut into ½-inch chunks

½ medium yellow bell pepper, seeded and cut into ½-inch chunks

1–2 jalapeño chiles or 1 hot red dried Chinese chile, seeded and minced

2 cups chicken broth

1 can (14 ounces) coconut milk

½ teaspoon salt

¼ teaspoon saffron threads

1 pound extra-large uncooked shrimp, shelled and deveined

2 tablespoons freshly squeezed lime juice

¼ cup minced fresh cilantro

1 Heat the oil over medium heat in a Dutch oven. Cook the shallots for 2 minutes, or until they begin to wilt. Add the garlic, ginger, and cumin. Stir. Add the rice. Continue cooking and stirring for several minutes.

2 Place the pumpkin chunks in a covered microwave-safe dish with 1 tablespoon water. Microwave on high for 5 minutes. Set aside to cool. When cool enough to handle, peel and cut into enough ½-inch chunks to make 2 cups.

3 Meanwhile, add the peppers and chiles to the shallot mixture and cook for 1 to 2 minutes before adding the broth, coconut milk, salt, and saffron. Bring to a boil, reduce the heat to low, and simmer for 35 to 40 minutes, until the rice is almost tender.

4 Add the shrimp and lime juice and cook 5 minutes longer, or until the shrimp turn pink and are thoroughly cooked.

5 Top each serving with a sprinkle of cilantro and serve.

FOR A MORE DRAMATIC PRESENTATION, serve in a cooked whole pumpkin. Choose a creamy Long Island Cheese, a blue-skinned Queensland, or a bright orange Cinderella. With a large knife, cut off the top and scoop out seeds and fibers with a large metal spoon. Rub the inside and outside lightly with oil and place the pumpkin and top on a jelly-roll pan. Bake in a 350°F oven for 30 minutes. Remove the top from the oven and bake the bottom of the pumpkin 15 minutes longer, or until it can be pierced with a fork, but does not collapse. The pumpkin should be able to stand on its own. The top should bake for only 30 minutes. When serving, scrape out a little pumpkin with each spoonful.

Ham and Cheese
Pumpkin Soufflé

SERVES 6

Cheese soufflé is a divine and airy delight that gains substance and flavor with the addition of ham and pumpkin.

3 tablespoons unsalted butter

¼ cup minced shallots

3 tablespoons unbleached all-purpose flour

1½ cups whole milk

1 cup canned unsweetened pumpkin

½ teaspoon dry mustard

½ teaspoon salt

¼ teaspoon ground nutmeg

¼ teaspoon dried thyme

2 eggs, separated, plus 3 egg whites

1½ cups grated sharp Cheddar

4 ounce slice of Danish deli ham, finely chopped (about 1 cup)

Softened butter for greasing soufflé dish

2 tablespoons dry breadcrumbs

1 Heat the oven to 375°F.

2 Melt the butter in a large heavy-bottomed saucepan over medium heat. Cook the shallots for 2 minutes over medium heat. Add the flour and cook over medium heat for 1 minute. Add the milk and continue cooking, until the mixture begins to boil and thicken. Boil for 1 minute. The sauce will be quite thick and a bit lumpy because of the shallots. Scrape the bottom of pan occasionally with a flat-ended wooden spoon.

3 Stir in the pumpkin, mustard, salt, nutmeg, and thyme. Beat the 2 egg yolks with a fork in a small bowl. Scrape the yolk mixture into the pan. Stir in the cheese and ham and cook, stirring constantly, over medium heat, until the sauce thickens. Remove from heat.

4 Beat the 5 egg whites in a bowl until they form stiff peaks. Stir one fourth of the egg whites into the pumpkin mixture. Fold the remaining egg whites into the mixture.

5 Grease the bottom and sides of a 2-quart straight-sided soufflé dish with butter. Sprinkle with the breadcrumbs.

6 Pour the soufflé mixture into the prepared dish. Run a finger around the top edge (to help the soufflé rise). Bake for 40 to 45 minutes, until it rises and is nicely browned.

Maple Glazed Ham
and Pumpkin

If you like candied sweet potatoes, you will love this. It is a great way to use up that roasted pumpkin that has been sitting in your freezer. Sweet and spicy is always good with ham and also with pumpkin. I love serving this with braised onions and kale or other strong greens.

SERVES 4

1 pound cured and fully cooked ham slice

2 cups leftover roasted pumpkin, cut into large chunks, or 1 pound fresh pumpkin, seeds and fibers removed, cut in chunks, and roasted (see pages 8–9)

¼ teaspoon dried thyme

1 tablespoon butter, melted

1 teaspoon salt

Freshly ground black pepper

1 can (8 ounces) pineapple chunks, rinsed and drained

¼ cup pure maple syrup

¼ cup orange juice

½ teaspoon ground cinnamon

¼ teaspoon dry mustard

1 Heat the oven to 325°F.

2 Quickly cook the ham on each side in a medium skillet over medium-high heat until it just begins to brown, about 1 minute on each side.

3 Grease a 1-quart shallow casserole dish with butter and lay the pumpkin in it. Coarsely mash the pumpkin, sprinkle with the thyme, drizzle with the butter, and season with the salt and pepper to taste.

4 Scatter the pineapple over the pumpkin and lay the ham slice on top. Mix together the maple syrup, orange juice, cinnamon, and mustard. Pour over everything and bake for 20 to 30 minutes, until the pumpkin is very soft and the ham lightly glazed.

5 Cut a wedge of ham and serve with a spoonful of pumpkin and a little juice.

Spicy Beef Stew in a *Pumpkin Shell*

The Greeks call their spicy beef stew stifado, which has been a favorite of my non-Greek family for years. It is one of the few stews I've come across where the tedious task of browning the meat is absent. Chunks of pumpkins are at home in this savory mix of tender beef, onions, tomato, and spices, which slowly cook undisturbed until serving time. Preparing the onions is a bit tedious, but fresh ones are so much tastier than canned or frozen that it is worth the effort. If time is a big factor, as it usually is, use three pounds of frozen pearl onions instead of the fresh ones. For a festive touch, this stew is served in a pumpkin.

SERVES 6

1 tablespoon butter

1 tablespoon olive oil

2 pounds stewing beef

1 teaspoon salt

Freshly ground black pepper

2 pounds small white onions

½ cup red wine

¼ cup tomato paste

2 tablespoons red wine vinegar

1 tablespoon brown sugar

1 clove garlic, minced

1 bay leaf

1 small cinnamon stick

6 whole cloves

1 tablespoon currants (optional)

¼ teaspoon ground cumin

1 pound fresh pumpkin, seeds and fibers removed, peeled, cut into ½-inch cubes (about 2 cups)

1 edible pumpkin, 4–5 pounds, for serving (Cinderella variety works well, and the bright orange color looks great)

1 Heat the butter and oil in a large Dutch oven over medium heat. Add the meat, salt, and pepper and stir with butter and oil just to coat, not to brown.

2 Cut off the root and stem ends of the onions. Make a small "x" in the root end to keep the onions from falling apart. Remove the skins and spread them over the meat. A quick way to loosen skins is to parboil the onions for 1 minute in a large saucepan of boiling water.

3 Mix the wine, tomato paste, vinegar, sugar, and garlic together and pour over meat and onions. Scatter the bay leaf, cinnamon, cloves, currants, if using, and cumin over the top. Bring the stew to a boil, reduce the heat, and simmer, covered, for 2 hours. Do not stir. Gently press the pumpkin into the stew. Cover and continue cooking for 1 hour longer, or until the meat is very tender.

4 Meanwhile, heat the oven to 350°F. Cut the top off of the pumpkin and scrape out the seeds and stringy insides. Rinse thoroughly and pat dry. Rub the outside with vegetable oil, place on a jelly-roll pan, and bake for 30 to 45 minutes, until easily pierced with a fork, but not collapsing. Set the hot pumpkin on a serving plate.

5 Spoon the hot stew into the hot pumpkin and scrape a bit of pumpkin with each serving of stew.

Tex-Mex Chili

A colorful, hearty dish, this chili, plus cornbread and a big green salad, is the perfect meal for a crowd. My friends from Cincinnati like their chili served with rice, chopped onion, and grated Cheddar. I think they are on to something.

SERVES 12

1 tablespoon olive oil

1 large onion, thinly sliced, about 2 cups

3 cloves garlic, minced

2 pounds ground beef

2 teaspoons salt

3 bell peppers (a mix of colors), seeded and cut into ½-inch chunks

2 jalapeño chiles, seeded and minced

1 pound white mushrooms, stemmed and quartered

2 pounds fresh pumpkin, seeds and fibers removed, peeled, cut into ½-inch chunks (about 4 cups)

2 cans (15 ounces each) red kidney beans, rinsed and drained

1 can (28 ounces) plum tomatoes with juice

1 can (8 ounces) tomato sauce

3–4 tablespoons chili powder

3 teaspoons ground cumin

Chopped onions, for topping

Grated Cheddar, for topping

1 Heat the olive oil in a large Dutch oven over medium heat. Add the onion and cook over medium-high heat for 5 minutes, or until onion wilts, stirring occasionally. Add the garlic and cook 1 minute longer.

2 Add the ground beef and cook and stir until it loses its red color, about 7 minutes. Sprinkle 1 teaspoon of the salt over the meat while stirring.

3 Add the peppers, chiles, mushrooms, and pumpkin. Reduce the heat to medium and continue cooking, stirring occasionally, for 15 to 20 minutes, until the pumpkin is easily pierced with a fork.

4 Add the kidney beans, tomatoes, tomato sauce, chili powder, cumin, and the remaining teaspoon salt. Cook 15 minutes longer. Taste and adjust the seasonings, if desired. Serve with bowls of chopped onions and grated cheddar for topping.

Meatloaf with Pumpkin Glaze

A classic meatloaf is hard to beat. Pumpkin is a natural at keeping the loaf together and adding a depth of flavor. The mildly sweet glaze on top is the perfect final touch. Add some carrots to the pan and throw some Russet potatoes alongside to roast with the meatloaf for one of the finest comfort meals around.

SERVES 8

1 slice whole wheat bread

2 tablespoons low-fat milk

½ cup finely chopped onion

¾ cup canned unsweetened pumpkin

¼ cup chopped fresh parsley

1 egg

1 tablespoon dried oregano

1 teaspoon salt

Freshly ground black pepper

2 pounds meatloaf mix (ground beef, pork, and veal)

2 tablespoons dark brown sugar

1 Heat the oven to 375°F.

2 Tear the bread into small pieces and place in a large bowl with the milk. Let it sit for a 1 to 2 minutes, until the bread absorbs the milk.

3 Add the onion, ½ cup of the pumpkin, the parsley, egg, oregano, salt, and pepper to taste, and whisk everything together.

4 Add the meat, stir with a wooden spoon, then mix thoroughly with your hands. Pat the mixture into a loaf shape and place in a shallow 2-quart casserole dish.

5 Whisk the remaining ¼ cup pumpkin with the brown sugar and spread on the top.

6 Bake for 1 hour. Let the loaf sit in pan for 10 minutes before slicing.

TIP: Almost better than meatloaf for dinner is a meatloaf sandwich for lunch, made with a thick slice between fresh whole wheat bread and served with coarse mustard and sweet pickles.

Punkin' Joes

My friend Julie serves a version of this barbecue beef at her Halloween party for kids. I've spiced it up and recommend serving it with fresh coleslaw. If you can find whole wheat hamburger buns, use them for the extra flavor, not to mention the fine nutrition.

SERVES 6

1 tablespoon canola oil

1 medium onion, thinly sliced (about 1½ cups)

1½ pounds lean ground beef

1 teaspoon salt

Freshly ground black pepper

1 cup canned unsweetened pumpkin

1 can (8 ounces) whole tomatoes and juice

1 can (8 ounces) tomato sauce

¼ cup chili sauce

2 tablespoons molasses

2 tablespoons cider vinegar

1 tablespoon chili powder

1 teaspoon ground cumin

¼ teaspoon hot sauce

6 whole wheat hamburger buns

1 Heat the oil in a Dutch oven over medium heat and cook the onion for 2 minutes, until soft. Add the ground beef and cook until it loses its red color, stirring and breaking it into small pieces as you cook. Add the salt and a few grinds of pepper.

2 Stir in the pumpkin, tomatoes, tomato sauce, chili sauce, molasses, vinegar, chili powder, cumin, and hot sauce. Bring to a boil, reduce the heat, partially cover, and cook for 45 to 50 minutes, or until the flavors blend and the mixture thickens. If it gets too thick, add a few tablespoons of water. Stir occasionally.

3 Just before serving, lightly toast the buns. Fill each bun with a generous scoop of Punkin' Joe.

Pork Tenderloin
with Red Wine Sauce

Choose a red wine with berry flavors for this rich, jammy sauce. Serve the tenderloins with Mashed Potatoes and Pumpkin (see page 62) and sautéed broccoli with garlic.

SERVES 6

1 tablespoon olive oil

2 pork tenderloins, about 1¼ pounds each

1 teaspoon salt
Freshly ground black pepper

4 cloves garlic, minced

1 tablespoon finely chopped fresh rosemary

½ cup red wine (preferably zinfandel or pinot noir)

¼ cup balsamic vinegar

3 tablespoons canned unsweetened pumpkin, or leftover pumpkin purée

2 tablespoons berry jam (strawberry, blackberry, blueberry, or raspberry)

1 tablespoon butter

1 Heat the oven to 350°F.

2 Heat the oil in a large skillet over medium-high heat. Rub the tenderloins with the salt and pepper.

3 Brown the tenderloins about 2 or 3 minutes on each side. Add the garlic and rosemary to the pan and roll the tenderloins around in the seasonings for several minutes. Set the skillet aside for later.

4 Place the tenderloins, garlic, and rosemary in a roasting pan and cook for 30 to 40 minutes, until the internal temperature reaches 165°F for 10 minutes. Slice the meat and arrange on a platter.

5 While the tenderloins are cooking, place the skillet over medium heat and add the red wine and vinegar. Cook until the liquid evaporates to about half. Add the pumpkin and jam and cook until the sauce thickens to the consistency of heavy cream. Swirl the butter into the sauce just before serving. Drizzle sauce over the slices of tenderloin.

Pork Stew
with Pumpkin and Prunes

Pork, pumpkin, and prunes are made for each other in this deep, rich blend of spices, meat, vegetables, and fruits that only gets better as the flavors continue to blend. I recommend making it a day ahead and serving it with brown rice and a salad with some bitter greens.

SERVES 6

2 tablespoons canola oil

2 pounds boneless pork loin, cut into 1-inch cubes

½–1 teaspoon salt

1 medium onion, thinly sliced (about 1½ cups)

3 cloves garlic, minced

1 teaspoon peeled and chopped fresh ginger

2 tablespoons unbleached all-purpose flour

1 cup chicken broth

1 cup apple cider

1 cup dark beer

1½ pounds fresh pumpkin, seeds and fibers removed, peeled, cut into ½-inch cubes (3–4 cups)

1½ cup pitted prunes, chopped

3 tablespoons cider vinegar

2 tablespoons Dijon mustard

2 whole cloves

1 cinnamon stick

1 bay leaf

1 teaspoon grated orange zest

1 Heat one tablespoon of the oil in a Dutch oven over medium heat. Add the pork in a single layer, sprinkle with the salt, and brown on all sides, about 5 to 10 minutes. Transfer the meat to a bowl with a slotted spoon and set aside.

2 Add the remaining oil to the pot and add the onion. Cook for 2 minutes before adding the garlic and ginger. Cook 1 minute longer. Return the pork to the pot, along with any juices that have accumulated in the bowl. Sprinkle with the flour, stir, and cook for 1 minute longer.

3 Add the chicken broth, cider, beer, pumpkin, prunes, vinegar, mustard, cloves, cinnamon, bay leaf, and orange zest. Bring to a boil, cover, and simmer for 1 hour. Stir occasionally. Taste, adjust the seasonings, if desired, and cook 15 minutes longer. If it is too soupy, leave the lid off for the last bit of cooking.

Apricot Stuffed Pork Tenderloin
with Pistachio Crust

Pork tenderloin lends itself to all kinds of wonderful ingredients. Pumpkin and apricot filling adds not only color, but a tangy sweetness to a dish topped off with the salty crunch of pistachios. For easy entertaining, prepare the tenderloin ahead except for the final cooking, and serve it with risotto and roasted green beans. You will find pumpkin butter in with jams and jellies in the supermarket, or make your own (see page 22).

SERVES 6

2 **pork tenderloins, about 1¼ pound each**

2 **teaspoons salt**

   Freshly ground black pepper

2 **tablespoons olive oil**

1 **medium onion, chopped (about 1½ cups)**

4 **cloves garlic, minced**

1 **tablespoon crumbled dried sage**

¼ **cup pumpkin butter**

¼ **cup goat cheese, softened**

½ **cup dried apricots (about 1½ ounces)**

½ **cup shelled pistachio nuts, finely chopped**

1 Butterfly each tenderloin by slicing horizontally almost through. Spread out each tenderloin on a cutting board and season with 1 teaspoon of the salt and a few grinds of pepper.

2 Heat the oven to 350°F.

3 Heat 1 tablespoon of the olive oil in a large skillet over medium heat. Cook the onion in the oil until soft, about 4 minutes. Add the garlic and cook 1 minute longer. Add the sage, the remaining teaspoon salt, and pepper to taste, and cook for 1 minute. Remove from the heat and put the skillet aside for later.

4 Spread one tablespoon of the pumpkin butter and half the onion mixture on one side of the inside of each tenderloin. Dot each with 2 tablespoons of the goat cheese. If the apricots are plump, slice them crosswise to make thin slices and arrange them on top of the filling. Close the tenderloins over the filling, press down, and tie with several 12-inch lengths of string. If some of the filling oozes out, brush it on top before roasting.

5 Heat the remaining tablespoon of the oil in the skillet over medium-high heat. Brown the tenderloins on all sides, turning after 2 to 3 minutes on a side.

6 Brush each tenderloin with remaining pumpkin butter, press most of the pistachios into the top and sides, and place them in a roasting pan to roast for 30 to 40 minutes, until the internal temperature is 165 degrees and the meat is nicely browned. Remove the pan from the oven, tent the tenderloins with aluminum foil, and let sit for 10 minutes.

7 Remove the string and slice the tenderloins. Arrange the slices on a platter and scatter the pan juices and reserved pistachios on top.

Armenian Lamb Stew
in a Pumpkin Shell

Bringing a bright orange pumpkin filled with the spicy aromas of this steaming stew to the table makes a spectacular presentation as you connect with this ancient cuisine. Apricots, which sweeten the spices, are a favorite ingredient in Armenian cooking. Scrape bits of pumpkin from the sides as you serve each portion over noodles, brown basmati rice, or polenta, or with Lavash, a flat bread typically wrapped around spicy meat and vegetables.

SERVES 8

1 tablespoon olive oil

2 pounds lamb stew meat, cut into 1-inch cubes

1 teaspoon ground coriander seeds

1 teaspoon ground cumin

½ teaspoon ground cardamom

1 teaspoon salt

1 large onion, thinly sliced (about 2 cups)

5 cloves garlic, minced

2 pounds fresh pumpkin, seeds and fibers removed, peeled, cut into ½-inch cubes (about 4 cups)

2 large carrots, peeled and cut into ¼-inch slices

1 cup peeled celery root, cut into ¼-inch dice

5 cups chicken broth

1 can (28 ounces) whole tomatoes with juice

5 whole cloves

1 cinnamon stick

½ cup dried apricots, chopped

1 Cinderella pumpkin, 7–8 pounds, with top cut off, seeds and fibers removed, washed, and brushed with oil (see pages 7–8)

½ cup minced fresh cilantro

1   Heat the oil in a large Dutch oven over medium-high heat. Combine the lamb with the coriander, cumin, and cardamom in a small bowl. Add half the seasoned lamb to the pot in a single layer. Cook the meat and spices for about 4 minutes, until the lamb is lightly browned and remove to a plate. Sprinkle with ½ teaspoon of the salt. Repeat with the remaining lamb.

2   Add the onion to the pot and cook for 5 minutes, until wilted, stirring occasionally. Add the garlic and cook for 1 minute longer. Add the pumpkin, carrots, and celery root, and cook for 1 to 2 minutes, until softened.

3   Return the lamb to the pot with the broth, tomatoes, cloves, and cinnamon stick. Bring to a boil and simmer, partially covered, for 1 hour 30 minutes, or until the lamb is tender. Add the apricots for the last half hour.

4   Meanwhile, heat the oven to 350°F.

5   Place the prepared large pumpkin on a jelly-roll pan.

6   Bake 40 to 45 minutes, until it can be pierced with a fork, but not collapsing because it has to hold the stew. The top should be added after 15 minutes so it bakes only 30 minutes.

7   Place the pumpkin on a large serving plate and fill with the hot stew. Serve hot and sprinkle each serving with cilantro.

Lamb Kebabs
with Red Peppers, Onions, and Pumpkin

SERVES 6

Present these kebabs on a white platter to show off the colors of grilled lamb chunks, pumpkin, red pepper, and onions. I always like a sauce with lamb, and this tangy yogurt mint sauce is perfect with these kebabs. Serve them with basmati rice or a simple pilaf and a salad of crisp greens for a fabulous buffet.

2½ pounds lamb shoulder chops, about ½-inch thick, cut into 1-inch pieces

MARINADE

¾ cups olive oil

1½ cups red wine vinegar

¼ cup minced shallots

¼ cup minced parsley

3 cloves garlic, minced

1 tablespoon Dijon mustard

1 tablespoon dried oregano

1 teaspoon dried thyme

2 pounds fresh, firm pumpkin, peeled, seeds and fibers removed, cut into 24 chunks, 1-inch each (about 4 cups)

1½ large sweet onions, trimmed, peeled and cut into eighths

1 large red bell pepper, seeded and cut into 1-inch chunks

YOGURT SAUCE

1 cup nonfat plain yogurt

1 tablespoon minced fresh mint leaves

1 teaspoon freshly squeezed lemon juice

1 Place the lamb in a low casserole dish.

2 To make the marinade, combine the oil, vinegar, shallots, parsley, garlic, mustard, oregano, and thyme in a medium bowl. Pour all but 2 tablespoons over the meat and toss to coat thoroughly. Place in the refrigerator for 1 hour. Save the reserved marinade for the vegetables.

3 Microwave the pumpkin in a few spoons of water for 30 seconds on high. Drain and place the pumpkin, onions, and pepper in a large bowl, toss with the remaining 2 tablespoons of the marinade, cover, and refrigerate for 30 minutes.

4 Heat the grill to high, then reduce the heat or move coals to one side. Assemble 6 skewers with an onion quarter at each end and pieces of lamb, pumpkin, and pepper arranged in between. If there are leftovers of meat or vegetables, make another skewer.

5 Grill for 5 to 10 minutes per side, until the meat is slightly firm and browned and the vegetables are crisp tender. Remove from the grill onto a serving platter.

6 To make the sauce, whisk all the ingredients together in a small bowl. Transfer to a small serving bowl and pass around with the kebabs.

TIP: If using bamboo skewers, use long ones, 12 to 18 inches, and soak them for 30 minutes before threading the food on them. For each kebab, use two skewers so the meat and vegetables won't spin around when you turn them. If using metal skewers, go for ones that are flattened, as they are less likely to spin. Sometimes I arrange skewers of meat separately from the vegetables. It doesn't look as beautiful as a skewer bursting with different colors and shapes, but it allows for different cooking times, if needed.

Thai Green Lamb Curry

Thai curries are flavored with mixes of herbs and spices, spiked with either yellow, red, or green chiles, green being the hottest. The many layers of flavor typical of Thai cooking are created by the blend of spices, coconut milk, cilantro, peanuts, and condiments. Go easy with the curry paste if you are unfamiliar with its heat. It is available in the Asian section of most supermarkets, or gourmet food stores. Serve with brown basmati rice. If using cooked lamb, follow the instructions, but reduce the cooking time to 15 minutes.

SERVES 4

½ pound fresh pumpkin, seeds and fibers removed, cut into chunks

2 tablespoons canola oil

1 small Chinese cabbage, chopped, about 1½ cups

1 stalk celery, chopped (about ½ cup)

1 medium onion, thinly sliced (about 1½ cups)

2 cloves garlic, minced

1 Granny Smith, or other tart apple, chopped

1–2 teaspoons Thai green curry paste

1 teaspoon peeled and grated fresh ginger

1½ teaspoons salt

1½ pounds boneless lamb stew meat, trimmed and cut into 1½-inch cubes, or 2 cups cooked lamb

1 cup coconut milk

2 tablespoons chopped fresh cilantro

½ cup chopped peanuts

CURRY CONDIMENTS

Mango Chutney

Dried currants

Shredded coconut

Nonfat plain yogurt

1 Heat the oven to 400°F.

2 Roast the pumpkin for 45 minutes, or until easily pierced with a fork. When cool enough to handle, peel and mash enough to make 1 cup. Store the rest in the refrigerator for up to 1 week, or in the freezer for up to 3 months.

3 Heat 1 tablespoon of the oil in a large skillet or sauté pan over medium heat. Add the cabbage, celery, onion, garlic, and apple and cook, stirring, for about 5 minutes. Stir in the curry paste. With a slotted spoon, remove the vegetables from the pan onto a plate.

4 Add the second tablespoon of the oil to the skillet over medium heat. Distribute the meat over the pan and cook at medium-high heat until the meat begins to brown, about 5 minutes.

5 Add the pumpkin and coconut milk to the pan, stirring to loosen the browned bits stuck to the bottom. Bring to a boil, reduce the heat, and simmer for 15 minutes. Return the vegetables to the pan and continue cooking for 15 to 20 minutes until the lamb is cooked and the vegetables are tender, but not mushy or overcooked. Stir in the cilantro and peanuts and serve with the condiments.

Braised Cabbage
with Sausage and Pumpkin

Here is a quick and easy one-dish dinner that will satisfy all palates. On a frosty winter night, get a good video and fill the house with the aroma of this simmering dish. Serve with extra mustard and parsley-boiled potatoes.

- 1 tablespoon olive oil
- 6 smoked chicken apple sausages, cut in half lengthwise
- 1 pound fresh pumpkin, seeds and fibers removed, cut into chunks
- 1 medium onion, sliced (about 1 cup)
- 3 cloves garlic, minced
- 1 head Napa cabbage, washed and sliced crosswise
- 1 tart apple, cored and thinly sliced
- ½ cup dry white wine
- 2–3 teaspoons Dijon mustard
- ½ teaspoon salt
- ⅛ teaspoon celery seed
- 1 cup chicken stock
- Freshly ground black pepper

1 Heat 1 teaspoon of the oil in a large skillet or sauté pan over medium-high heat. Add the sausages and brown them lightly, about 5 minutes. Remove from pan and set aside.

2 Microwave the pumpkin on high for 5 minutes. When cool enough to handle, remove the skin, and coarsely chop enough to make 2 cups. Store the rest in the refrigerator for up to 1 week, or in the freezer for up to 3 months.

3 Heat the remaining oil in pan, add the onion and garlic and cook for several minutes, until softened. Add the cabbage. Cook and stir until the cabbage begins to wilt, about 5 minutes. Add the pumpkin, apple, wine, mustard, salt, and celery seed. Add enough stock to simmer everything without sticking to the pan.

4 Cover and cook for 8 minutes, or until the cabbage and apples are tender. Add the sausages and a few grinds of pepper, and simmer a few minutes to warm the sausages. Taste and adjust the seasonings.

Spaghetti with
Peppers, Onions & Sausage

Peppers and onions just belong together. Add some pumpkin and sausage to make a spicy sauce that can be poured over spaghetti for a simple meal. Add a loaf of bread and nice red wine for a perfect dinner.

SERVES 4

4   **sweet Italian sausages**

1   **pound fresh pumpkin, seeds and fibers removed, cut into chunks**

1   **tablespoon olive oil**

1   **medium onion, thinly sliced, 1 ½ cups**

1   **red bell pepper, seeded and sliced**

1   **green bell pepper, seeded and sliced**

1   **teaspoon salt**

   Freshly ground black pepper

1   **teaspoon dried oregano**

1   **can (14.5 ounces) plum tomatoes with juice**

½   **cup red wine**

   Dash of red pepper flakes

1   **pound spaghetti**

½   **cup freshly grated Parmesan, for serving**

1   Turn the grill to high. When hot, reduce the heat to medium and grill the sausages until brown all over, about 10 minutes. Remove from the grill and slice into ½-inch slices. Set aside.

2   Heat the oven to 400°F. Rub the pumpkin chunks with oil, place in a roasting pan, and cook for 45 minutes, or until easily pierced with a fork. When cool enough to handle, remove the skin and coarsely chop enough to make 2 cups. Store the rest in the refrigerator for up to 1 week, or in the freezer for up to 3 months.

3   Heat the oil in a large skillet over medium heat and cook the onion in the oil for about 5 minutes, or until soft. Add the red pepper and green pepper and continue cooking.

4   Mix the pumpkin with the salt, pepper to taste, and oregano and add to the skillet. Add the sausages, tomatoes, and wine. Bring to a boil, stirring constantly. Reduce the heat and simmer for about 20 minutes, until the sauce thickens. Season with the pepper flakes.

5   While the sauce is cooking, cook the spaghetti until al dente. Drain, divide among 4 plates, spoon the sauce over each plate, and pass the Parmesan.

Northern Italian
Pumpkin Lasagna

Homemade lasagna is always a labor of love, and this is not different, although using no-cook noodles cuts out one step. This is another pasta dish in which tomatoes make no appearance, as is typical of Northern Italian pastas. Instead a creamy béchamel sauce separates the layers of pasta, pumpkin, and cheese. Accompany with a salad of crisp greens. If using regular noodles, cook and drain them and reduce the amount of sauce. Use 4 tablespoons butter, 5 tablespoons flour, and 4 cups milk.

SERVES 8

1 tablespoon butter

1 tablespoon olive oil

1 large onion, thinly sliced (about 2 cups)

2 pounds fresh pumpkin, seeds and fibers removed, peeled and chopped (about 4 cups)

1 tablespoon oregano

1 teaspoon salt

Freshly ground black pepper

½ pound bulk sweet Italian chicken sausage

1 large clove garlic, minced

1 Heat the butter and oil in a large sauté pan or skillet over medium heat. Add the onion and cook for 5 minutes, or until wilted.

2 Stir in the pumpkin and cook for 10 minutes, stirring occasionally. Season with the oregano, the salt, and a few grinds of pepper. Add the sausage and cook until it loses its color, about 5 minutes. Stir in the garlic and cook for 1 minute longer. Set aside.

3 Meanwhile, make the sauce. Melt the butter in a large heavy-bottomed saucepan over medium heat. Add the flour. Cook for 1 minute, until bubbly. Whisk in the milk and cook, stirring, until mixture thickens and bubbles, about 5 minutes. Add the salt, pepper, and nutmeg, and set aside.

4 Combine the two cheeses in a medium bowl.

5 Heat the oven to 375°F.

BÉCHAMEL SAUCE

- 5 tablespoons butter
- 6 tablespoons unbleached all-purpose flour
- 5 cups nonfat milk
- ½ teaspoon salt
- ¼ teaspoon white pepper
- ¼ teaspoon ground nutmeg
- 3 cups grated part-skim mozzarella
- 1½ cups freshly grated Parmesan
- 12 oven ready/no boil lasagna noodles

6 To assemble the lasagna, spray a 9- by 13- by 2-inch baking pan with nonstick cooking spray. Ladle ¾ cup of sauce on the bottom of the pan and top with 3 noodles, placed crosswise.

7 Pour another ¾ cup of sauce over the noodles, then ⅓ of the pumpkin filling. Sprinkle 1 cup of the cheese mixture over the filling. Repeat the layers of sauce, noodles, filling, and cheese twice. Top this with the remaining noodles, pour over the remaining sauce, and sprinkle with the remaining cheese. The lasagna should look soupy.

8 Spray a sheet of aluminum foil with nonstick spray and cover the top of the pan, with the oiled side facing down. Bake for 45 minutes, uncover, and baking 10 to 15 minutes, or until lightly browned and bubbly. Let the lasagna sit for 15 minutes before cutting and serving.

Creamy Fusilli, Sausage, and Pumpkin

SERVES 6

A creamy pumpkin sauce envelops coils of fusilli. I thank my niece, Maura, for this very satisfying combination. Enjoy it with the remaining white wine, steamed baby peas, and a big green salad.

2 tablespoons olive oil

1 pound bulk sweet Italian sausage

1 medium onion, thinly sliced

4 cloves garlic, minced

1 bay leaf

2 tablespoons fresh sage, chopped

1 cup dry white wine

1 cup chicken broth

1 cup canned unsweetened pumpkin

½ cup heavy cream

½ teaspoon ground nutmeg

½ teaspoon salt

Freshly ground black pepper

1 pound fusilli pasta, or bow-tie pasta

6 tablespoons shaved Parmesan

1 Heat one tablespoon of the olive oil in a large skillet over medium heat. Add the sausage, and cook for 5 minutes, or until the red color is gone. Remove from the skillet and drain. Wipe out the skillet.

2 Heat the remaining tablespoon of olive oil over medium heat and add the onion. Cook for 3 minutes, until softened. Add the garlic and continue cooking for 3 minutes, or until the onion and garlic are soft and beginning to brown.

3 Add the bay leaf, sage, and wine to the pan. Bring to a boil, then reduce the heat. Do not cover. Simmer and stir to scrape up the browned bits until the wine is reduced by half, about 5 minutes.

4 Whisk in the broth and pumpkin and bring to a low boil while stirring. Stir in the cream, add the sausage, and cook over low heat for several minutes. Add the nutmeg, salt, and pepper to taste. Adjust the seasonings, if necessary.

5 Meanwhile, cook the pasta until al dente. Drain and add the pasta to the skillet. Toss the sauce and pasta together while cooking over low heat for 1 to 2 minutes.

6 Top with the Parmesan and serve.

BREADS

A lovely shade of pale orange colors, the quick breads in this chapter bear little resemblance to the pasty palette of most such breads. Mixed with dried fruits, nuts, citrus, and spices, pumpkin brings a rich element to these breads. Start your day with delicate scones, crunchy biscotti, or moist coffeecake. Complete the day with a cup of tea accompanied by a thin slice of one of the many pumpkin breads.

Hazelnut-Pumpkin Biscotti
Iced with Chocolate

Fragrant with cardamom, colored with pumpkin, and iced with chocolate, these crunchy hazelnut biscotti await a dunk in a cup of strong espresso. A well-kept secret is that biscotti are quite simple to make, store very well, and make fabulous little gifts.

MAKES 30 PIECES

1 cup hazelnuts

½ cup (1 stick) unsalted butter, softened

1 cup sugar

3 eggs

1 teaspoon vanilla extract

½ cup canned unsweetened pumpkin

3 cups unbleached all-purpose flour

1 teaspoon baking powder

½ teaspoon ground cardamom

½ teaspoon salt

¼ teaspoon ground allspice

¼ teaspoon ground nutmeg

6 ounces semi-sweet chocolate chips (about 1 cup)

1 Heat the oven to 350°F.

2 Spread the hazelnuts on a jelly-roll pan and bake for 20 minutes, or until lightly toasted. Remove them from the oven and pour onto a clean kitchen towel. When cool, rub them with the towel to remove most of the skins, and coarsely chop.

3 Beat together the butter, sugar, eggs, and vanilla in a large bowl until light and fluffy. Blend in the pumpkin.

4 Sift the flour, baking powder, cardamom, salt, allspice, and nutmeg together into the creamed mixture and continue beating until well combined. Stir in the hazelnuts.

5 Refrigerate the mixture in the bowl for at least 2 hours, as it will be sticky.

6 Again, heat the oven to 350°F.

7 Divide the dough into 2 mounds and turn one out onto a floured board. With floured fingers, shape into 2 loaves, ½- by 3-inches wide. Place the loaves on a parchment-lined cookie sheet, leaving about 4 inches between them for expansion.

8 Bake for 35 to 40 minutes, until they are golden brown. Cool on a wire rack.

9 Reduce the oven to 300°F.

10 Slice the loaves diagonally and place cut-side down on the cookie sheet. Bake 15 to 20 minutes per side or until dried out. Cool on wire racks.

11 While the biscotti are cooling, melt the chocolate in a small heavy-bottomed saucepan over very low heat. Spread the hot chocolate on the top and sides of one end of each biscotti. Set them on a wire rack until the chocolate is set. Store in a loosely covered container for up to two weeks.

Almond-Pumpkin Biscotti

MAKES 30 PIECES

Pumpkin turns this basic biscotti a peachy shade of orange. While physical therapist Elsie Limm was working on my neck and shoulder, we got talking about pumpkin recipes. She offered many great ideas, including this simple and elegant biscotti recipe.

¾ cup (1½ sticks) unsalted butter, softened

2 cups dark brown sugar

3 eggs

1 teaspoon vanilla extract

¾ cup canned unsweetened pumpkin

3 cups unbleached all-purpose flour

1 tablespoon ground cinnamon

1 teaspoon ground allspice

1 teaspoon baking powder

1 teaspoon ground ginger

½ teaspoon salt

¼ teaspoon ground nutmeg

1½ cups almonds, coarsely chopped

1 Beat together the butter, brown sugar, eggs, and vanilla in a large bowl until light and fluffy. Stir in the pumpkin.

2 Sift the flour, cinnamon, allspice, baking powder, ginger, salt, and nutmeg together into the creamed mixture and continue beating until well mixed. Stir in the almonds.

3 Refrigerate the mixture in the bowl for at least 2 hours.

4 Heat the oven to 350°F. Line a cookie sheet with parchment.

5 Divide the dough into 2 mounds and turn one out onto a floured board. With floured fingers, shape into 2 loaves, ½- by 3-inches wide. Place the loaves on the cookie sheet, leaving about 4 inches between them for expansion. Bake for 35 to 40 minutes, until golden brown. Cool on a wire rack.

6 Reduce the heat to 300°F.

7 Slice the loaves diagonally and place cut-side down on the cookie sheet. Bake 15 to 20 minutes per side, or until dried out.

8 Cool completely and store in a loosely covered container for up to two weeks.

Currant-Pumpkin-Oat Scones

MAKES 8

A brunch of warm, fragrant scones, a bowl of fresh berries, steaming coffee, and the Sunday papers is a most delightful way to begin the day.

1½ cups unbleached all-purpose flour

¾ cup rolled oats

¼ cup sugar

1 tablespoon baking powder

1 teaspoon ground cinnamon

¼ teaspoon salt

4 tablespoons (½ stick) cold unsalted butter

½ cup dried currants

1 egg

½ cup unsweetened canned pumpkin

2 tablespoons heavy cream

1 Heat the oven to 350°F.

2 Place the flour, oats, sugar, baking powder, cinnamon, and salt in the bowl of a food processor and quickly pulse. Add the butter and pulse until the mixture resembles coarse crumbs, about 30 seconds. Pour the mixture into a large bowl and mix in the currants.

3 Combine the egg, pumpkin, and cream in a small bowl and add to the flour mixture. Stir with a fork until the flour is moistened.

4 Turn the dough onto a floured board and knead a few times, then pat it into a 1-inch circle. Slice it into 8 equal wedges and place each on an ungreased baking sheet. Bake for 20 to 25 minutes, or until lightly browned. Serve warm as is, or with butter and jam.

Lemon-Pumpkin-Cranberry
Scones

Treat your weekend guests to buttery scones studded with cranberries, hot from the oven before heading off for your day's activities. For a variation, use lime or orange zest.

MAKES 12

3¼ cups unbleached all-purpose flour

¾ cup sugar

1 teaspoon baking powder

½ teaspoon salt

3 tablespoons lemon zest

½ cup (1 stick) unsalted butter, cold, cut into small pieces

1½ cups fresh cranberries, chopped

2 eggs, slightly beaten

½ cup canned unsweetened pumpkin

¼ cup heavy cream

¼ teaspoon ground nutmeg

1 Heat the oven to 350°F.

2 Place the flour, ½ cup of the sugar, baking powder, salt, and lemon zest in the bowl of a food processor and quickly pulse. Add the butter and pulse until the mixture resembles coarse crumbs, about 30 seconds.

3 In a small bowl, mix the cranberries with the remaining ¼ cup sugar and add to the flour mixture. Pulse a few times to mix everything and pour into a large bowl.

4 Combine the eggs, pumpkin, cream, and nutmeg in the small bowl and add to the flour–cranberry mixture. Stir with a fork until the flour is moistened.

5 Turn the dough onto a floured board and knead a few times, then pat into a 1-inch-thick circle. Slice into 12 equal wedges and place on an ungreased cookie sheet.

6 Bake for 15 to 20 minutes, or until lightly browned. Serve warm with honey.

TIP: For smaller scones, pat the dough into 2 circles and cut each into 8 pieces. Check after 15 minutes.

Chocolate Chip Pumpkin Bread

Basic pumpkin bread is delicious, but isn't everything enhanced with chocolate? I don't often think of bread for dessert, but try this as a sweet ending to a simple meal. Serve with coffee or tea.

MAKES 2 LOAVES

4 **eggs**

1¾ **cups sugar**

1½ **cups canned unsweetened pumpkin**

1 **cup canola oil**

3 **cups unbleached all-purpose flour**

2 **teaspoons baking powder**

1 **teaspoon baking soda**

1 **teaspoon ground cinnamon**

1 **teaspoon ground ginger**

1 **teaspoon salt**

¼ **teaspoon ground nutmeg**

2 **cups chopped walnuts or pecans (optional)**

1½ **cups semi-sweet chocolate chips**

1 Heat the oven to 350°F.

2 Whisk the eggs, sugar, pumpkin, and oil in a large bowl until thoroughly blended.

3 Sift the flour, baking powder, baking soda, cinnamon, ginger, salt, and nutmeg into the pumpkin mixture. Fold in the nuts, if using, and chocolate chips.

4 Divide batter between two greased 8- by 4- by 2-inch pans. Bake 75 to 80 minutes, or until a skewer inserted in the center comes out clean. Cool on a rack for at least 10 minutes before removing from pan. Cool completely before slicing.

TIP: This is a terrific bake-sale item or a house gift. It can be double wrapped in plastic wrap and stored in the freezer for up to 3 months.

Half Moon Bay
Pumpkin Bread

Kathy Ellis, an innkeeper in Half Moon Bay, California, served this rich, spicy bread to us. A little research revealed that this classic bread is an old family recipe from Kris Mason, one of the organizers of the annual Half Moon Bay Arts and Pumpkin Festival in the California central coastline region. It is the best basic pumpkin bread I've tasted, with its crunchy top and moist inside. Spread a thin layer of cream cheese on a slice and sit down with a cup of afternoon tea. If you have a spare loaf of this bread, let it dry out and turn it into bread pudding.

MAKES 1 LOAF

1 cup canned unsweetened pumpkin

1 cup sugar

½ cup canola oil

2 eggs

1¾ cups unbleached all-purpose flour

1 teaspoon baking soda

½ teaspoon ground cinnamon

½ teaspoon ground cloves

½ teaspoon ground nutmeg

½ teaspoon salt

¼ teaspoon baking powder

1 cup nuts (walnuts or pecans), chopped

1 Heat the oven to 350°F. Grease an 8- by 4-inch loaf pan.

2 Beat together the pumpkin, sugar, oil, and eggs in a large bowl.

3 Sift the flour, baking soda, cinnamon, cloves, nutmeg, salt, and baking powder into the bowl. Stir to combine all the ingredients. Fold in the nuts. Pour into the prepared pan.

4 Bake for 60 minutes, or until the top is lightly browned and a skewer inserted into the center comes out clean. Cool on a wire rack. Either enjoy it right away or double wrap in plastic wrap and store in the freezer for up to 3 months.

Cranberry~Orange~ Pumpkin Bread

Orange and cranberry is another combination of sweet and tart that gets the juices flowing. Add a little pumpkin, and you have a most satisfying breakfast bread which will brighten any brunch table.

MAKES 2 LOAVES

2 cups sugar

¾ cup (1½ sticks) unsalted butter, softened

4 eggs

2 cups canned unsweetened pumpkin

1 tablespoon grated orange zest

Juice of one orange (about ½ cup)

3½ cups unbleached all-purpose flour

2 teaspoons baking powder

2 teaspoons ground cinnamon

1 teaspoon ground nutmeg

1 teaspoon salt

½ teaspoon baking soda

1½ cups walnuts, chopped

1½ cups dried cranberries

1 Heat the oven to 350°F. Grease two 8- by 4-inch pans with butter.

2 Beat the sugar and butter in a large bowl until fluffy. Add the eggs, pumpkin, and zest. Add enough water to the orange juice to make ⅔ cup. Add to the sugar mixture and continue beating until well blended.

3 Sift the flour, baking powder, cinnamon, nutmeg, salt, and baking soda into the pumpkin mixture.

4 Fold in the nuts and cranberries.

5 Divide the batter between the two pans. Bake 70 to 80 minutes, or until a skewer inserted in the middle comes out clean and the top is golden brown. Cool on a rack for at least 10 minutes before removing from the pan. Cool completely before slicing. Serve immediately or double wrap in plastic wrap and store in the freezer for up to 3 months.

Banana-Pumpkin-Nut Bread

MAKES 2 LOAVES

This dense, subtly flavored bread is yummy on its own, or toasted and slathered with pumpkin butter for breakfast.

1 cup canola oil

1½ cups sugar

½ cup dark brown sugar

2 ripe bananas, peeled and mashed (1 cup)

1½ cups canned unsweetened pumpkin

4 eggs, slightly beaten

2 tablespoons freshly squeezed orange juice

1 tablespoon grated orange zest

3½ cups unbleached all-purpose flour

2 teaspoons baking powder

2 teaspoons cinnamon

1 teaspoon ground ginger or 2 teaspoons peeled, grated fresh ginger

1 teaspoon salt

½ teaspoon allspice

¼ teaspoon baking soda

2 cups coarsely chopped walnuts or pecans

½ cup raisins (optional)

1 Heat the oven to 350°F. Grease two 8- by 4- by 2-inch pans with butter.

2 Beat the oil and sugars in a large bowl until thoroughly blended. The mixture will look grainy. Add the banana, pumpkin, eggs, orange juice, and orange zest, and continue beating until well blended. Sift the flour, baking powder, cinnamon, ginger, salt, allspice, and baking soda into the pumpkin mixture.

3 Fold in the nuts and raisins, if using.

4 Divide the batter between the two prepared pans. Bake 80 to 90 minutes, or until a skewer inserted in the middle comes out clean and the top is golden brown. The top will crack and get crusty. Cool on a rack for at least 10 minutes before removing from pan. Cool completely before slicing. Serve immediately or double wrap in plastic wrap and store in the freezer for up to 3 months.

TIP: This is a terrific bake-sale item or a house gift.

Pumpkin Cornbread

This fabulous tea bread is not too sweet, but the cornmeal makes it interesting enough to disappear quickly. My friend Toni shared this recipe with me. It is simple to make and oh, so easy to eat. Serve as a tea bread or toasted lightly for breakfast.

MAKES 1 LOAF

1⅓ cups unbleached all-purpose flour

1 cup ground cornmeal

1 cup sugar

2 teaspoons baking powder

1 teaspoon ground cinnamon

½ teaspoon baking soda

¼ teaspoon salt

2 eggs

1 cup canned unsweetened pumpkin

4 tablespoons unsalted butter, melted

½ cup nonfat milk

¾ cup walnuts, coarsely chopped

1 tablespoon honey mixed with 1 tablespoon melted butter (optional, to brush on baked loaf)

1 Heat the oven to 350°F. Grease a 9- by 5-inch loaf pan with oil.

2 Combine the flour, cornmeal, sugar, baking powder, cinnamon, baking soda, and salt in a large bowl, until thoroughly mixed.

3 Whisk together the eggs, pumpkin, butter, and milk in a smaller bowl. Quickly mix this into the flour mixture until just combined. Gently stir in the walnuts.

4 Pour the batter into the prepared pan. Bake for 50 to 60 minutes, or until the loaf is golden brown and slightly separated from the edge of the pan, and a skewer inserted into the center of the loaf comes out clean. Remove from the oven and cool on a wire rack for 10 minutes. Remove from the pan and brush with the glaze, if using. Cool completely before slicing with a serrated knife.

Date-Nut-Pumpkin Muffins

MAKES 12 MUFFINS

Some muffins are a little side attraction to eat with something else. Chock full of dates and nuts, rich with pumpkin and spice, each of these dense, flavorful muffins is worthy of being the center of attention.

2 eggs

1 cup canned unsweetened pumpkin

½ cup (1 stick) unsalted butter, melted

1 cup dates, pitted and chopped

½ cup walnuts, chopped

1¾ cups unbleached all-purpose flour

¾ cup sugar

1 teaspoon baking powder

1 teaspoon ground cinnamon

¼ teaspoon ground allspice

¼ teaspoon baking soda

¼ teaspoon ground nutmeg

¼ teaspoon salt

Pinch of mace

1 Heat the oven to 350°F. Grease 12 muffin cups.

2 Whisk together the eggs, pumpkin, and butter in a large bowl. Stir in the dates and walnuts.

3 Sift the flour, sugar, baking powder, cinnamon, allspice, baking soda, nutmeg, salt, and mace into the pumpkin mixture. Using a rubber spatula, mix in the flour mixture until it is just moistened.

4 Evenly distribute the batter into the muffin cups. Bake for 20 to 25 minutes. Cool on a wire rack for 15 minutes. Remove from the pan and cool completely on a wire rack, or serve warm.

Spicy Cranberry Pecan
Pumpkin Muffins

MAKES 1½
DOZEN LARGE
MUFFINS, *or*
3 DOZEN SMALL
MUFFINS

Packed with flavorful goodies, these muffins will brighten your morning. Serve a batch to your weekend guests or to friends for brunch. Tuck them into your kids' lunchboxes. Make a double batch and double wrap and freeze the extra for up to 2 months.

1 cup dried cranberries, chopped

2 eggs

½ cup brown sugar

½ cup canola oil

½ cup canned unsweetened pumpkin

½ cup plain nonfat yogurt

½ cup chopped pecans

6 tablespoons granulated sugar

1 teaspoon peeled, grated fresh ginger

2¼ cups unbleached all-purpose flour

1 tablespoon ground cinnamon

1 teaspoon baking powder

½ teaspoon baking soda

½ teaspoon salt

¼ teaspoon ground nutmeg

1 Heat the oven to 350°F. Grease 18 muffin cups (or 36 if small), or use paper liners.

2 Whisk together the cranberries, eggs, brown sugar, oil, pumpkin, yogurt, pecans, granulated sugar, and ginger in a large bowl.

3 Sift the flour, cinnamon, baking powder, baking soda, salt, and nutmeg into the pumpkin mixture. Quickly mix, until the flour is moistened. Divide the batter among the muffin cups.

4 Bake for 25 to 30 minutes, or until lightly browned on top and a skewer inserted into the center of a muffin comes out clean. Cool on a wire rack, or serve while still warm.

Pumpkin Doughnut Muffins

MAKES 24
MUFFINS

Inspired by The Classic Zucchini Cookbook, *these muffins originate from the Downtown Bakery and Creamery in Healdsburg, California. These delightful concoctions are rolled in cinnamon and sugar.*

1 cup sugar

½ cup (1 stick) unsalted butter, softened

2 eggs

1¾ cups canned unsweetened pumpkin

¼ cup buttermilk

3 cups unbleached all-purpose flour

1 tablespoon baking powder

1 teaspoon baking soda

1 teaspoon salt

¼ teaspoon ground nutmeg

TOPPING

½ cup sugar

2 teaspoons ground cinnamon

4 tablespoons butter, melted

1 Heat the oven to 350°F

2 Beat the sugar and butter together in a large bowl until fluffy. Add the eggs, one at a time, beating after each. Beat in the pumpkin and buttermilk.

3 Sift the flour, baking powder, baking soda, salt, and nutmeg into the pumpkin mixture, beating until smooth. The batter will be stiff.

4 Spray two 12-cup muffin pans with butter-flavored spray. Divide the batter among the 24 cups and bake for 25 to 30 minutes, or until the muffins are golden brown and a tester comes out clean. Cool the muffins for a few minutes on a wire rack.

5 For the topping, mix the sugar and cinnamon. When the muffins are cool enough to handle, generously brush the tops with butter and roll in the cinnamon and sugar. Cool on the wire rack and serve.

◆ ◆ ◆

Variation

For mini-muffins, brush the entire muffin and roll in the cinnamon and sugar. It's messy, very rich, and tasty.

◆ ◆ ◆

Pumpkin Popovers

MAKES 12
POPOVERS

For years, I taught seventh graders to make popovers, which are so simple, so elegant, and yet a delicious surprise that never fails to delight. A subtle hint of pumpkin and spice adds enormously to the pleasure. Serve hot and dripping with butter, along browned breakfast sausages.

4 eggs

1¾ cups nonfat milk

3 tablespoons oil

¼ teaspoon ground allspice

¼ cup canned unsweetened pumpkin

1½ cups unbleached all-purpose flour

1 tablespoon sugar

¼ teaspoon salt

1 tablespoon butter, cut into 12 small pieces

◆ ◆ ◆

Variation

For a savory version, omit the sugar and allspice. Add ¼ teaspoon ground cumin and fill the cooked popovers with curried chicken salad. Add some Parmesan to the batter to make it even richer.

◆ ◆ ◆

1 Heat the oven to 450°F.

2 Place a 12-cup muffin pan, or two 6-cup popover pans, in the oven while it warms.

3 Whisk the eggs, milk, oil, allspice, and pumpkin in a medium bowl.

4 Sift the flour, sugar, and salt into the egg mixture and stir until well blended. The batter will be the consistency of very heavy cream.

5 Remove the pans from oven, drop a piece of butter in each cup, and evenly divide the batter among the cups.

6 Bake for 20 minutes, without peeking, and reduce the heat to 350°F. Continue baking for 20 minutes, or until the popovers are browned and crisp on the outside. They should be able to hold their shape and yet be soft on the inside. Remove them from the oven, pierce the top of each, and dump onto a wire rack. Serve hot.

Lemon-Cranberry-Pumpkin
Coffee Cake

MAKES ONE
9-INCH CAKE

I just love the combination of pumpkin and cranberry, both the colors and flavors.

2 cups unbleached all-purpose flour

1 teaspoon baking powder

1 teaspoon baking soda

½ teaspoon salt

1 cup granulated sugar

½ cup (1 stick) unsalted butter, softened

2 eggs

1 teaspoon vanilla extract

1 tablespoon lemon juice

¾ cup plain nonfat yogurt

¾ cup canned unsweetened pumpkin

1 teaspoon grated lemon zest

¾ cup dried cranberries

½ cup light brown sugar

½ cup walnuts, coarsely chopped

2 teaspoons ground cinnamon

1 teaspoon ground allspice

1 Heat the oven to 350°F. Grease a 9-inch tube pan.

2 Sift together the flour, baking powder, baking soda, and salt in a medium bowl. Set aside.

3 Beat the granulated sugar and butter together in a large bowl until fluffy. Add the eggs, vanilla, and lemon juice and beat until very light.

4 Mix the yogurt, pumpkin, and lemon zest together in a small bowl. Add some of the flour to the butter mixture and then add some of the yogurt mixture. Mix well and repeat until everything is combined in one bowl.

5 Stir in all but 2 tablespoons of the cranberries. Pour half the batter into the prepared pan.

6 Mix the remaining ingredients together in a medium bowl. Sprinkle half the mix on the batter. Spread the remaining batter over this, and sprinkle the remaining topping and cranberries over all.

7 Bake for 45 to 55 minutes, or until a skewer inserted into the center comes out clean.

8 Cool on a wire rack for 10 minutes before removing from the pan.

Orange-Pumpkin Pancakes

On Sunday mornings, we serve these incredibly smooth and mellow pancakes with warm maple syrup for a sensational start to the day. One secret to making perfect pancakes is having the griddle hot enough to brown, but not hot enough to burn the pancakes. The other secret is to cook the pancakes on the first side until little bubbles appear on the top, to be sure the pancakes are cooked.

MAKES 12 PANCAKES

1 cup whole wheat pastry flour (if unavailable, use unbleached all-purpose flour)

1 teaspoon baking powder

½ teaspoon ground cinnamon

½ teaspoon salt

¾ cup orange juice

½ cup canned unsweetened pumpkin

¼ cup canola oil

2 eggs

Pure maple syrup, for serving

Butter, for serving

1 Heat the oven to 200°F.

2 Combine the flour, baking powder, cinnamon, and salt in a large bowl.

3 Whisk together the orange juice, pumpkin, oil, and eggs in a small bowl and stir into the flour mixture until you have a smooth batter.

4 Meanwhile, heat a large griddle over medium to medium-high heat. When a drop of water dances on the griddle, it is hot enough. The griddle shouldn't smoke, but it needs to be hot. You may have to reduce the heat if the bottoms get too dark before the tops are cooked through.

5 Spoon about ¼ cup of batter for each pancake onto the hot griddle. Cook until the little bubbles form, then quickly flip the pancakes to the other side. Cook until just browned on the second side. Place on a serving plate and set in the oven while making the rest of the pancakes. Serve with the Sunday papers.

Pumpkin-Walnut Biscuits

Sweetly spiced, these pumpkin-colored and -flavored biscuits are a perfect accompaniment to omelets or eggs of any persuasion. Brighten a brunch table with a basket filled with these steaming beauties. For a savory note, replace the sugar with grated Parmesan and substitute ¼ to ½ teaspoon thyme, savory, or tarragon for the spice mix.

MAKES 16

1½ cups unbleached all-purpose flour

½ cup whole wheat pastry flour (see page 169)

¼ cup sugar

4 teaspoons baking powder

½ teaspoon ground allspice

½ teaspoon ground cinnamon

½ teaspoon ground nutmeg

½ teaspoon salt

½ cup (1 stick) butter, cut into small pieces

⅓ cup walnuts, chopped

1 cup canned unsweetened pumpkin

1 Heat the oven to 400°F.

2 Combine flours, sugar, baking powder, allspice, cinnamon, nutmeg, and salt together in a food processor. Add the butter and pulse a few times, until the mixture resembles coarse crumbs.

3 Dump the mixture into a large bowl and stir in the nuts. Stir in the pumpkin and mix until the dry ingredients are just moistened. Scrape the dough onto a floured surface and knead a few times, adding a little more flour if it is very sticky.

4 Pat the dough into a ½-inch-thick circle and cut biscuits with a 2-inch biscuit cutter. Form the scraps into another ½-inch round and continue cutting biscuits.

5 Place the biscuits 1 inch apart on a baking sheet and bake for 12 to 15 minutes, until risen and lightly browned.

PIES

*N*ot everyone loves pumpkin pie like I do, but everyone knows that pumpkin pie is a longstanding tradition on the Thanksgiving table. A spicy, light, custardy pumpkin filling nestled in a flaky crust and topped with a generous dollop of whipped cream is the perfect ending to the turkey-with-all-the-trimmings meal. Thus this chapter begins with a recipe for a fabulous, no-frills pumpkin pie. This mother recipe is followed by many variations, which purists may disdain, but which those not wild about the original may find intriguing, not to mention yummy. I hope there is something here for everyone.

THE PUMPKIN

John Greenleaf Whittier (1807–1892)

. . . Ah! On Thanksgiving day, when from East and from West,
From North and from South come the pilgrim and guest,
When the gray-haired New Englander sees round his board
The old broken links of affection restored,
When the care-wearied man seeks his mother once more.
And the worn matron smiles where the girl smiled before,
What moistens the lip and what brightens the eye?
What calls back the past, like the rich pumpkin pie?

Oh, fruit loved of boyhood! The old days recalling,
When wood-grapes were purpling and brown nuts were falling!
When wild, ugly faces we carved in its skin,
Glaring out through the dark with a candle within!
When we laughed round the corn-heap, with hearts all
in tune,
Our chair a broad pumpkin, our lantern the moon,
Telling tales of the fairy who travelled like steam,
In a pumpkin-shell coach, with two rats for her team!

The thanks for thy present! None sweeter or better
E're smoked from the oven or circles in platter!
Fairer hands never wrought at a pastry more fine,
Brighter eyes never watched o're its baking, than thine!
And the prayer, which my mouth is too full to express,
Swells my heart that thy shadow may never be less,
That the days of thy lot may be lengthened below,
And the fame of thy worth like a pumpkin-vine grow,
And thy life be as sweet, and its last sunset sky
Golden-tinted and fair as thy own Pumpkin pie!

Sweet Pumpkin

THE RECIPES FOR SWEET PUMPKIN DISHES use an ever-changing blend of spices. Cinnamon is always a winner, but I like using mixes of other spices to blend with the mildly sweet flavor of pumpkin. Experiment and find your own favorite combinations and quantities from the list below. Proceed gradually because you can always add more spices, but it is hard to remove them. My favorite story of overdoing spices was the seventh grader who read only "¼" and quickly tossed ¼ cup of cinnamon into a small pot of applesauce instead of ¼ teaspoon. You can imagine the result.

Spices that go well with pumpkin

- Ground allspice
- Ground cardamom
- Ground cinnamon
- Ground cloves
- Fresh grated or ground ginger
- Ground nutmeg

Pumpkin Pie Spice

You can make a basic spice mix for pumpkin pie by mixing the following spices together and storing them in an airtight container, using about 2 teaspoons for a 9-inch pie.

- ¼ cup ground cinnamon
- 1 tablespoon ground ginger
- 2 teaspoons ground nutmeg
- 1 teaspoon ground cloves

Vary the amounts of these spices according to your taste buds. Substitute ground allspice and ground cardamom for the cloves and nutmeg. When you find the mix you love, use it in some of the recipes in this book.

Piecrust Pastry Dough

MAKES TWO 9-
INCH PIECRUSTS,
or ONE 9- OR 10-
INCH DOUBLE-
CRUST PIE

Carefully wrap and store unused dough in the freezer for up to a month. Thaw in the refrigerator and then let it sit out for a half hour before rolling out.

- 3½ cups unbleached all-purpose flour
- 1 teaspoon salt
- ½ cup cold unsalted butter, cut into small pieces
- 1 cup vegetable shortening, chilled and cut into small chunks
- ⅔ cup ice water

1 Sift the flour and salt into a large bowl. Mix in some of the butter with a pastry blender. Add the remaining butter and continue mixing until the mixture looks like coarse crumbs. Alternatively, you may quickly press the flour into the butter between your thumbs and fingers or pulse it in a food processor, leaving some chunks.

Add the shortening and continue to work the dough until it is distributed throughout in small lumps.

2 Add a bit of the water and work it into the mixture with a fork (don't do this in the food processor). Add more to a dry place and work it in. Continue in this fashion until the water is gone and the dough is formed. Don't overwork it. Don't use the food processor for adding water because it is too easy to overmix.

3 Form the dough into 2 balls, flatten them, wrap them in plastic, and refrigerate for about 2 hours. The dough can stay in the refrigerator for several days. If you want to freeze the whole thing, divide it in half and double wrap each piece or store in a plastic freezer bag.

4 Let the dough sit out for a half hour before you roll it. Place a flattened disk of dough on a lightly floured board or pastry cloth. Starting in the center, roll to the edges as if you were forming the spokes of a wheel. Check to make sure the dough isn't sticking to the board. Lift dough gently and keep rolling until 10- to 11-inches in diameter, or a little bigger than your pie pan. Place it in the pie pan and trim the excessive overhang, leaving enough to fold the outer edge under to rest on the rim of the pan. Crimp the edge between your thumb and forefinger all the way around, building it up as you go.

5 Refrigerate the dough for about 30 minutes before filling.

For a partially baked crust, heat the oven to 400°F. Place a sheet of aluminum foil in the bottom of the crust. Place pie weights or about 1½ cups of dried beans in the foil. Bake for 10 minutes. Remove the weights. Cool on a wire rack and proceed with your recipe.

For a fully baked crust, heat the oven to 400°F. Place a sheet of aluminum foil inside the crust. Fill with pie weights or 1½ cups dried beans. Bake for 10 minutes. Remove the foil and weights, prick the bottom and sides of the crust with a fork, and bake 7 to 10 minutes longer, until golden brown. Check for puffiness. If the crust has risen up, carefully poke it with a fork to release the air. Cool on a wire rack and proceed with your recipe.

Traditional Pumpkin Pie

This is the best pumpkin pie I've ever had. The recipe is inspired by Louise Andrews Kent in the guise of Mrs. Appleyard in an old Vermont cookbook. Concentrating and caramelizing the pumpkin before baking the pie is Mrs. Appleyard's secret to the rich flavor and creamy texture of this most traditional fall dessert. To follow a New England tradition, serve it with a slice of sharp Vermont Cheddar cheese instead of with whipped cream.

The secret of a tender, flaky piecrust is not to overmix the dough once the water is added. My mom always said she made the best pie crust when she was in a hurry. It is one of those recipes with a few simple ingredients that must be put together with great care.

**MAKES ONE
9-INCH PIE**

- 2 teaspoons butter
- 1 cup canned unsweetened pumpkin
- 2 tablespoons unbleached all-purpose flour
- 2/3 cup sugar, plus 2 tablespoons
- 2 cups milk
- 2/3 cup heavy cream
- 1 teaspoon peeled and grated fresh ginger
- 1/2 teaspoon ground cinnamon
- 1/4 teaspoon ground nutmeg
- 1/4 teaspoon salt
- 2 eggs, beaten
  Partially baked 9-inch piecrust (see page 153)

1 Melt 1 teaspoon of the butter in a heavy skillet over medium heat. Add the pumpkin and cook until the moisture is reduced and the pumpkin is lightly browned, about 5 minutes. You will have about ¾ cup smooth, thick, and slightly caramelized pumpkin.

2 Heat the oven to 450°F.

3 Sprinkle 1 tablespoon of the flour over the browned pumpkin in a large bowl and stir in ⅔ cup of the sugar.

4 Grease the bottom of a medium saucepan with the remaining teaspoon of the butter and heat the milk over medium heat until little bubbles form around the edges. Pour the milk, cream, ginger, cinnamon, nutmeg, and salt over the pumpkin and stir until well combined. Mix in the eggs.

- 1 cup heavy cream
- 1 tablespoon confectioners' sugar
- ¼ teaspoon ground cinnamon

5 Mix together the remaining 1 tablespoon flour and 2 tablespoons of the sugar in a small bowl and sprinkle in the bottom of the piecrust. Pull out the oven rack and place the piecrust in the oven. Pour the filling into it and carefully push the rack back into the oven. Bake 15 minutes.

6 Reduce the oven to 325°F and bake 30 minutes longer. The pie should jiggle slightly in the middle when it is done.

7 To make the topping, beat the cream until soft peaks form. Fold in the confectioners' sugar and cinnamon, and serve with the pie.

Pumpkin Rugalach

These bite-size Jewish cookies are traditionally made with cream cheese dough, but I make them with leftover piecrust. Fillings range from poppy seed paste to nuts to jam, and for these I've put in some pumpkin.

Heat oven to 400°F. Gather all leftover dough scraps and form into a ball. Roll into an oval. Spread a thin layer of softened butter over the dough. Mix 1 tablespoon canned pumpkin with 1 tablespoon sugar and ¼ teaspoon ground cinnamon. Spread this over the butter. Starting with the wide edge, tightly roll the dough. Diagonally cut in 1-inch slices and bake for 10 to 15 minutes, until lightly browned. Cool and nibble on them while you are cleaning up.

Date-Nut Pumpkin Pie

Nothing can beat a really good traditional pumpkin pie, but for those who like change, dates and nuts provide a texture to this old favorite.

To toast the walnuts, heat the oven to 350°F and place them on a baking sheet for 2 to 3 minutes, or until fragrant and lightly browned. Alternatively, toast them in a toaster oven set at 350°F for 5 minutes, or until fragrant.

**MAKES ONE
9-INCH PIE**

1 cup canned unsweetened pumpkin

2 tablespoons unbleached all-purpose flour

⅔ cup sugar, plus 2 tablespoons

1 teaspoon butter

2 cups milk

⅔ cup heavy cream

½ teaspoon salt

¼ teaspoon ground cardamom

¼ teaspoon ground cloves

2 eggs, beaten

1 cup dates, chopped

½ cup walnuts or pecans, chopped and toasted

Partially baked 9-inch piecrust (see page 153)

TOPPING

1 cup heavy cream

1 tablespoon confectioners' sugar

1 teaspoon pure vanilla extract

1 Lightly brown the pumpkin in a heavy skillet over medium heat until the moisture is reduced, and pumpkin appears dry, about 5 minutes. Remove to a large bowl.

2 Heat the oven to 450°F.

3 Sprinkle 1 tablespoon of the flour over the concentrated pumpkin and stir in ⅔ cup of the sugar.

4 Grease a medium saucepan with the butter and heat the milk over medium heat until little bubbles form around the edge. Pour the scalded milk, cream, salt, cardamom, and cloves over the pumpkin and whisk together until well combined. Mix in the eggs, dates, and nuts.

5 Stir the remaining 1 tablespoon of flour and 2 tablespoons sugar together in a small bowl and sprinkle in the bottom of the piecrust. Place the piecrust in the oven and pour filling into it. Bake 15 minutes.

6 Reduce the oven to 325°F and bake 30 minutes longer. The pie should jiggle slightly in the middle when it is done.

7 To make the topping, beat the cream until soft peaks form. Fold in the sugar and vanilla, and serve with the pie.

Southern Pecan Pumpkin Pie

MAKES ONE
9-INCH PIE

On the Outer Banks of North Carolina in Bubba's Restaurant, I had a fabulous sweet potato pecan pie made by "Mrs. Bubba." I can't get that pie out of my mind. This is the closest I've come to recreating that memory, using cooked fresh pumpkin that is lightly mashed instead of sweet potato. To gild the lily, serve with vanilla ice cream or whipped cream.

- 2 **cups chopped pecans**
- 1 **pound fresh pumpkin, seeds and fibers removed, cut into chunks**
- 3 **eggs**
- 1 **cup dark brown sugar**
- ¾ **cup dark corn syrup**
- 3 **tablespoons unsalted butter, melted**
- 2 **tablespoons bourbon**
- 1 **teaspoon salt**
- ½ **teaspoon ground cinnamon**
- ¼ **teaspoon ground nutmeg**
  Partially baked 9-inch piecrust (see page 153)

1 Heat oven to 350°F.

2 Spread the pecans on a baking sheet and toast for 5 to 7 minutes, until lightly browned and fragrant. Cool on a wire rack.

3 Microwave the pumpkin on high for 5 minutes, or until easily pierced with a fork. When cool, peel and cut into enough 1-inch chunks to measure 2 cups. Mash slightly.

4 Increase the heat to 375°F.

5 Whisk together the eggs, sugar, corn syrup, butter, bourbon, salt, cinnamon, and nutmeg in a large bowl. Add the cooled pecans and pumpkin. Spoon into the piecrust.

6 Bake 35 to 45 minutes, until the filling is set. Cool for at least 1 hour 30 minutes before slicing.

Meringue Pumpkin Pie

𝒜 rich and creamy layer lightly topped with meringue makes a heavenly dessert. My friend Judy's mom, Beulah, provided the inspiration for this delightful version of pumpkin pie. Instead of covering the filling with meringue, fold the beaten egg whites into the custard to create a chiffon pie using a graham cracker crumb crust.

**MAKES ONE
9-INCH PIE**

1 package (.25 ounces) unflavored gelatin

1 cup sugar

¾ cup nonfat milk

¾ cup canned unsweetened pumpkin

1 teaspoon freshly squeezed lemon juice

½ teaspoon ground cardamom

Pinch of salt

3 eggs, separated

½ cup heavy cream

Fully baked 9-inch piecrust (see page 153)

¼ teaspoon cream of tartar

1 Heat the oven to 375°F.

2 Whisk together the gelatin, ⅔ cup of the sugar, milk, pumpkin, lemon juice, cardamom, and salt in a medium heavy-bottomed saucepan.

3 Stirring constantly with a flat-bottomed wooden spoon, bring the mixture to a boil over medium-high heat and cook until it begins to thicken, 3 to 5 minutes. Whisk the egg yolks in a small bowl and add a little of the hot mixture to them. Return the yolks to the pot, reduce the heat, and cook, stirring, for 2 to 3 minutes, to thicken further. Don't let the mixture boil. Remove from the heat.

4 (For best results, refrigerate the bowl, beaters, and heavy cream until cold before proceeding.) Beat the heavy cream in a medium bowl until soft peaks form. Fold the whipped cream into the pumpkin filling and pour it all into the cooled pie shell. Set the pie in the preheated oven.

5 Beat the egg whites and cream of tartar in a medium bowl until soft peaks form. Continue beating and slowly add the remaining ⅓ cup sugar in a thin stream. Beat until stiff peaks form and the whites are glossy but not dry.

6 Remove the pie from the oven and spread the meringue over the hot pie filling, starting with a band around the crust. Next fill in the center, so the entire pie is covered with meringue. Touch the meringue with the back of a large spoon in random places to form decorative peaks. Bake for 10 to 12 minutes, or until the meringue is browned.

7 Cool thoroughly on a rack before slicing. This pie is best served the day it is made, but if that isn't possible, store it in the refrigerator overnight.

Spicy Pumpkin Ice Cream Pie
with Gingersnap Pecan Crust

**MAKES ONE
9-INCH PIE**

Cool and creamy, crunchy and spicy, this sensational and simple dessert has it all. Katherine Phillips, who shared her recipe with me, traces it to her native Minnesota. Candied ginger is sold in the spice aisle of most grocery stores.

CRUST

- 9 **gingersnaps, 2 inches in diameter**
- 1 **cup pecans, finely chopped**
- ¼ **cup sugar**
- 2 **tablespoons minced candied ginger**
- 4 **tablespoons butter, softened**

FILLING

- 1 **cup canned unsweetened pumpkin**
- ½ **cup brown sugar**
- ½ **teaspoon ground cinnamon**
- ½ **teaspoon ground ginger**
- ¼ **teaspoon ground nutmeg**
- 1 **quart creamy French vanilla ice cream, slightly softened, but not melted**

1 Heat the oven to 425°F.

2 To make the crust, put the gingersnaps in a sturdy plastic bag and roll them with a rolling pin until finely crumbled. Reserve 1 tablespoon of the crumbs and pour the rest into a medium bowl. Mix in the pecans, sugar, and ginger. With a fork or your fingers, mash in the butter until the mixture is thoroughly combined and crumbly.

3 Spread the crumbs into a 9-inch pie pan to cover the bottom and sides. With a flat-bottomed glass, pat the bottom of the crust to pack it down, or place an 8-inch pie dish on top and press down. Bake for 5 to 7 minutes, or until lightly browned. Remove from the oven and cool on a wire rack.

4 To make the filling, stir together the pumpkin, sugar, cinnamon, ginger, and nutmeg in a medium bowl, until smooth. Fold the ice cream into the pumpkin mixture until the color is uniform. Spread the filling into the cooled crust and sprinkle with the reserved crumbs. Freeze for 3 to 4 hours, or until firm. Cover the pie with aluminum foil and store for up to 1 week. Let pie sit out for 15 minutes before slicing and serving.

Oat Crumb Crust

For a nice variation, try a different crumb crust for this pie:

1⅓ cups of old-fashioned oats, uncooked

⅓ cup of firmly packed brown sugar

1 teaspoon ground cinnamon

5 tablespoons unsalted butter, melted

Heat the oven to 350°F. Combine the oats, sugar, cinnamon, and butter in a small bowl, mixing until crumbly. Firmly press onto bottom and sides of a 9-inch pie pan. Bake for about 8 minutes, or until lightly browned. Cool and fill.

Pumpkin-Pear *Galette*

Galettes are sometimes called rustic tarts because they don't strive for the perfection of a pie, but are equally delicious and simpler to make. The pears in this rich dough are accompanied by pumpkin, some spice, a bit of sweetness, and a hint of lemon for an impressively delicious pastry. This is a perfect dessert for fall, when the pears are ripe and masses of pumpkins are available. You could also experiment with other varieties of sweet pears, such as red Anjou, or crisp sweet apples.

SERVES 6–8

RICH PASTRY CRUST

- **1 cup unbleached all-purpose flour**
- **1 teaspoon sugar**
- **¼ teaspoon salt**
- **6 tablespoons butter**
- **2 tablespoons vegetable shortening**
- **¼–⅓ cup ice water**

1 To make the crust, stir the flour, sugar, and salt together in a medium bowl. Cut the butter into small pieces and drop into bowl. Toss to coat and work the butter into flour with a pastry blender, until pieces resemble tiny peas. Add the shortening and continue cutting into the mixture until the texture is like breadcrumbs, with some pea-sized pieces. Add the water bit by bit and mix in with a fork. Don't overmix. The dough should be moist enough to stick together when pressed. Wrap in plastic wrap and refrigerate for several hours. This dough can be kept in the refrigerator for 2 days or stored in a freezer bag in the freezer for up to 1 month.

2 To proceed with galette, heat the oven to 425°F.

3 Roll out the dough to a 13-inch circle on a lightly floured surface. Carefully loosen the dough and lift to a large jelly-roll pan.

FILLING

- 6 tablespoons canned unsweetened pumpkin
- 2 tablespoon brown sugar
- ½ teaspoon ground cinnamon
- ¼ teaspoon ground nutmeg
- ½ pound fresh pumpkin, seeds and fibers removed, peeled and grated (about 1 cup)
- 2 large ripe Bartlett pears, or 3 medium ones, peeled, cored, and cut into 1-inch slices
- ¼ cup sugar
- 1 teaspoon freshly squeezed lemon juice
- 1 teaspoon grated lemon zest
- 1 tablespoon apricot jam
- 2 tablespoons confectioners' sugar

❖ ❖ ❖

Variation:

Substitute 6 tablespoons pumpkin butter for the canned pumpkin, brown sugar, cinnamon, and nutmeg. If edible pumpkins are not available, peel and grate butternut squash.

❖ ❖ ❖

4 Combine the canned pumpkin with the brown sugar, cinnamon, and nutmeg in a small saucepan and cook over low heat for about 5 minutes, until the pumpkin loses some of its moisture. Stir frequently and cool slightly.

5 Leaving 1½-inches around the edge, spread the pumpkin mixture in a circle over the center of the dough.

6 Scatter the grated pumpkin over the pumpkin mixture.

7 Combine the pears with the granulated sugar, lemon juice, and lemon zest in a medium bowl. Pile them on top of the pumpkin and fold the edge of the dough around the filling. Don't worry if it ruffles; it is supposed to.

8 Bake for 20 minutes. Meanwhile, heat the jam on high in the microwave for 10 seconds.

9 Reduce the heat to 350°F. Brush the crust with the jam and continuing baking 20 to 30 minutes longer, until crust is lightly browned and the pears are soft when pierced.

10 Cool on a wire rack and then shake the confectioners' sugar over the crust.

Pumpkin Chess Pie

**MAKES ONE
9-INCH PIE**

This classic Southern pie is only enriched by the addition of pumpkin. For a tarter variation, substitute lemon zest for the orange zest and 2 tablespoons lemon juice for the orange juice.

¾ cup sugar

½ cup canned unsweetened pumpkin

¼ cup half-and-half

¼ cup freshly squeezed orange juice

3 eggs

2 tablespoons unsalted butter, melted

2 teaspoons grated orange zest

½ teaspoon vanilla extract

¼ teaspoon salt

⅛ teaspoon ground cardamom

1 tablespoon cornmeal

Partially baked 9-inch piecrust (see page 153)

TOPPING

1 cup heavy cream

3 tablespoons confectioners' sugar

1 Heat the oven to 375°F.

2 Whisk together the sugar, pumpkin, half-and-half, orange juice, eggs, butter, zest, vanilla, salt, and cardamom in a large bowl.

3 Sprinkle the cornmeal on the bottom of the piecrust. Pour in the filling and bake for 35 minutes, or until a knife inserted in the center comes out clean. Cool on a wire rack.

4 To make the topping, whip the cream until soft peaks form. Add the sugar and beat until the whipped cream mounds gently. Spread on the cooled pie and serve at room temperature or chilled.

COOKIES

Who can resist a cookie? These small-sized sweets are a perfect snack or accompaniment to coffee, or dessert in itself. It is sometimes hard to just eat one delicious cookie. They are fun to make and a great activity for little children. At age three, my granddaughter started "helping" me make cookies by dumping the measured ingredients into a bowl, stirring, cutting out cookies from rolled dough, and scattering "finkles" on the top.

When baking cookies, put only one cookie sheet in the oven at a time so the heat can circulate and bake the cookies evenly. Use two baking sheets. Put one in the oven and fill the second one while you are waiting. Pop it in the oven as soon as the first one comes out.

I usually line the baking sheets with parchment paper if I have it, but my preference is to use a silicon baking mat to cover the baking sheet. It keeps the bottoms nicely browned, the cookies come off easily, and it is reusable. If greasing the baking sheets, I use a cooking spray or the butter wrapper. In these recipes I suggest preparing the baking sheets with parchment paper (available in supermarkets along with waxed paper). If you have a silicon mat, use it instead. For bar cookies, I use a cooking spray. As with so many things, there are many options. Do what is easiest for you.

Halloween

On All Hallows Eve, the souls of the dead rise from their graves and visit the warmth and comfort of their old homes. Folks in those homes did not welcome the visit and dressed up in costumes to scare away the ghosts. They left treats at the door to appease the ghosts and carved out turnips with faces and lights to remind the spirits of the damned soul. The Irish brought these traditions and superstitions to America in the mid-19th century during the Potato Famine. They found that pumpkins were much more available than turnips, and thus we carve pumpkins and light them up on All Hallows Eve.

Pumpkin-Molasses Snaps

These chewy, spicy delights are the closest to perfection I've found on my quest for the perfect molasses spice cookie. Esther Christensen, my friend Jane's mom, used to make them with bacon grease, which was delicious, but I'm sticking to good old butter. Pumpkin makes them a little moister, which only adds to the essential texture and flavor that I so love.

MAKES 2½ DOZEN

½ cup (1 stick) unsalted butter, softened

1 cup sugar, plus ¼ cup for rolling

⅓ cup canned unsweetened pumpkin

¼ cup molasses

1 egg

2⅓ cups unbleached all-purpose flour

2 teaspoons baking soda

1 teaspoon ground cinnamon

1 teaspoon ground ginger

½ teaspoon ground cloves

½ teaspoon salt

1 Beat the butter in a large bowl. Add 1 cup of the sugar, pumpkin, molasses, and egg to the butter and continue beating until the mixture is well combined and fluffy.

2 Sift the flour, baking soda, cinnamon, ginger, cloves, and salt into the pumpkin mixture. With an electric or hand mixer at low speed, beat until the flour is thoroughly incorporated into the batter. Refrigerate for up to an hour, or until the batter can be handled.

3 Heat the oven to 350°F.

4 Place the remaining ¼ cup sugar in a pie pan. Form the batter into balls the size of a walnut, roll them in the sugar, and arrange on an ungreased cookie sheet, 2 inches apart. Bake 10 minutes, or until the cookies look cracked.

5 Cool for a few minutes on a wire rack before removing the cookies from the pan. Continue cooling on wire racks. Store in a cookie jar. These cookies will keep up to 3 months in the freezer, if not eaten before they make it to the freezer.

Pumpkin-Currant Cookies

Children love them. Maybe it is the orange color, the sweet bits of currant, or the crunch of macadamia nuts, but whatever it is, they disappear fast. To gild the lily, mix some confectioners' sugar into fresh lemon juice for a thin glaze to spread on the cookies.

MAKES 4 DOZEN

¾ cup (1½ sticks) unsalted butter, softened

1 cup sugar

1 egg

1 cup unsweetened canned pumpkin

2 cups unbleached all-purpose flour

1 teaspoon ground cinnamon

½ teaspoon baking powder

½ teaspoon salt

¼ teaspoon ground nutmeg

¼ teaspoon ground cloves

1 cup dried currants

1 cup macadamia nuts, coarsely chopped

1 Heat the oven to 350°F. Line two baking sheets with parchment paper.

2 Beat the butter and sugar together with a whisk or electric mixer until fluffy. Add the egg and pumpkin and continue beating until smooth.

3 Sift the flour, cinnamon, baking powder, salt, nutmeg, and cloves into the bowl and beat at low speed. Stir in the currants and nuts.

4 Drop the batter by tablespoons onto the prepared baking sheets, 2 inches apart. Wet your fingers and flatten the cookies a bit. Bake for 10 to 12 minutes, or until lightly browned around the edges.

5 Cool the baking sheets on a wire rack for a few minutes before removing the cookies from the sheet. Cool them completely on wire racks and store in a cookie jar that is not airtight.

TIP: Cookies bake more evenly and completely when only one pan is in the oven at a time. It prolongs the process, but the improved results are worth it.

Oatmeal-Chocolate Chip *Crisps*

They are not low fat and not low carb, but they are packed with flavor and satisfaction. These chewy morsels cry out for a tall glass of ice-cold milk.

MAKES 5 DOZEN

1 cup brown sugar

¾ cup granulated sugar

1 cup (2 sticks) unsalted butter, softened

½ cup canned unsweetened pumpkin

2 eggs

1 teaspoon vanilla extract

1½ cups unbleached all-purpose flour

1 teaspoon baking powder

1 teaspoon salt

½ teaspoon ground cinnamon

3 cups rolled oats

1½ cups semi-sweet chocolate chips

1 Heat the oven to 350°F. Line two baking sheets with parchment paper.

2 Beat the sugars and butter together with a hand mixer until well blended and fluffy. Add the pumpkin, eggs, and vanilla and beat until smooth.

3 Sift the flour, baking powder, salt, and cinnamon into the mixture and continue beating at low speed until well blended. Stir in the oats and chocolate chips.

4 Drop by tablespoons onto the prepared baking sheet. Bake for 12 to 15 minutes, or until lightly browned.

5 Cool the baking sheet on a wire rack for a few minutes before removing the cookies. Cool them completely on wire racks and store in an airtight container. Enjoy!

❖ ❖ ❖

Variation

If available, substitute some of the flour with whole wheat pastry flour. This is a low gluten flour that adds nutrition, but not the heaviness of whole wheat bread flour. It is a wonderful product to use in pastries and baked goods where you want the nutrition of whole wheat, but not the heaviness.

❖ ❖ ❖

Jack~o'~Lantern Cookies

A basic sugar cookie with a ghoulish grin on the lemon-flavored, bright orange icing makes a Halloween treat to delight the kids and grown-ups.

COOKIES

- **1** cup (2 sticks) unsalted butter, softened
- **¾** cup sugar, superfine if available
- **1** teaspoon vanilla extract
- **2½** cups unbleached all-purpose flour
- **¼** teaspoon salt

1 To make the cookies, heat the oven to 350°F. Line two baking sheets with parchment paper.

2 Beat together the butter, sugar, and vanilla until thoroughly blended and somewhat fluffy. Sift in the flour and salt and continue beating at low speed until the flour is completely mixed into the butter.

3 Scrape the dough onto a board and knead a few times before forming into 2 flat disks. Wrap the disks in plastic and refrigerate for 30 minutes.

4 Roll the dough to a thickness of ⅛-inch on a lightly floured surface. Using a large pumpkin cookie cutter or a biscuit cutter, cut out cookies and place them on the prepared baking sheet. Bake for 8 to 10 minutes, or until golden brown around the edges.

5 Cool the baking sheet on a wire rack for a few minutes before removing the cookies. Cool them completely on wire racks.

ICING

1 egg white, or 1 teaspoon powdered egg whites mixed with 2 tablespoons water

1 teaspoon grated lemon zest

1 tablespoon freshly squeezed lemon juice

2–2½ cups sifted confectioners' sugar

Orange food coloring

Licorice strings, cinnamon drops, and gumdrops, for making faces

6 To make the icing, beat the egg white until foamy and add the lemon zest and lemon juice. Gradually add the sugar and continue beating until the mixture reaches a consistency appropriate for spreading. Add a few drops of orange food coloring.

7 When the cookies are cool, spread a thin layer of icing over each one. Get some kids to help make the faces, or just leave as unadulterated pumpkins. Let the icing set before packing the cookies in an airtight container.

Maple-Pumpkin Pops
with Lemon Icing

These are pretty cute as well as tasty, and if I hadn't been hanging around with preschoolers, I never would have known about putting soft cookies on a popsicle stick for a bake sale. Lemon icing helps the grown-ups get past the garish pumpkin face to enjoy the flavors of this spicy, moist cookie with crispy edges.

MAKES 2 DOZEN

½ cup (1 stick) unsalted butter, softened

½ cup granulated sugar

⅓ cup pure maple syrup

½ cup canned unsweetened pumpkin

1 egg

1 teaspoon vanilla extract

1½ cups unbleached all-purpose flour

1 teaspoon baking powder

1 teaspoon ground ginger

½ teaspoon baking soda

½ teaspoon salt

⅛ teaspoon ground cumin

24 popsicle sticks (available in craft stores)

1 cup confectioners' sugar

1 tablespoon freshly squeezed lemon juice

Orange food coloring

¼ cup mini chocolate chips

1 Heat the oven to 350°F. Line two baking sheets with parchment paper.

2 Beat together the butter, granulated sugar, and syrup with a hand mixer, until light and fluffy. Add the pumpkin, egg, and vanilla, and beat until smooth.

3 Sift the flour, baking powder, ginger, baking soda, salt, and cumin into the bowl and beat until well combined. The dough will be soft but not sticky.

4 Drop by tablespoons 2 inches apart onto the prepared baking sheet. With a popsicle stick, perfect the circle shape of each cookie. Bake for 15 minutes.

5 Cool the baking sheet on a wire rack for a few minutes before removing the cookies. Cool completely on wire racks before icing. When cool, insert a popsicle stick horizontally halfway in each cookie.

6 When the cookies are cool, decorate by mixing the confectioners' sugar and lemon juice together in a small bowl. Lightly color with the orange food coloring and spread a thin layer on each cookie. Use the mini chocolate chips to make jack-o'-lantern faces on each cookie. Serve to your favorite ghosts and goblins or take to the harvest bake sale.

◆ ◆ ◆

Variation

These cookies serve equally well for other holidays. Try this Fourth of July version. Divide the icing into three bowls and color one white, one red, and one blue. With a thin knife, make a diagonal stripe on each cookie. Continue by making a red stripe above the white and a blue stripe below.

◆ ◆ ◆

Graham Cracker
Pumpkin Tannies

A hint of spice and a bit of pumpkin make one of my favorite bar cookies into something special.

MAKES 3 DOZEN

27 graham cracker squares, rolled into crumbs (about 2½ cups)

¼ teaspoon ground allspice

1 can (14 ounces) sweetened condensed milk

½ cup canned unsweetened pumpkin

1 teaspoon vanilla extract

1 package (6 ounces) semi-sweet chocolate chips

½ cup walnuts, coarsely chopped

½ cup unsweetened coconut (optional)

NOTE: Sweetened condensed milk is a lot thicker and sweeter than evaporated milk. Don't confuse them.

1 Heat the oven to 350°F. Spray a 9-inch square pan with cooking spray.

2 Combine the crumbs and allspice in a large bowl. Add the condensed milk, pumpkin, and vanilla and mix well. Stir in the chocolate chips, nuts, and coconut, if using.

3 Spread the batter evenly in the prepared pan. Bake for 35 minutes, or until lightly browned on top and pulling away from sides of pan.

4 Cool on a wire rack for only 5 minutes before cutting into squares. Then cool completely and store in an air-tight container.

TIP: Place the graham crackers in a plastic bag and whack them with a rolling pin to break them into large pieces. Roll them in the bag until they make coarse crumbs. An alternative is to pay more and buy graham cracker crumbs.

Chocolate-Pumpkin Brownies
with Apricot Surprise

MAKES 24 BROWNIES

Maybe it is because they are both orange, but pumpkin with apricot is a fabulous combination. When chocolate is added, the combination is truly memorable. I like to cut these very rich brownies into 1-inch squares and serve them with coffee or milk, depending on the audience.

5 ounces unsweetened baking chocolate

½ cup (1 stick) unsalted butter

2 cups sugar

3 eggs

1½ cups canned unsweetened pumpkin

1 cup unbleached all-purpose flour

1 teaspoon salt

1 teaspoon ground ginger

1½ cups chopped pecans

¾ cup apricot jam

1 Heat the oven to 350°F. Spray a 9- by 13-inch baking pan with cooking spray.

2 Melt the chocolate and butter in a large heavy-bottomed saucepan over low heat. Stir frequently and remove the pan from the heat when they are almost melted. Add the sugar and stir well.

3 Beat in the eggs and then the pumpkin. When mixture is smooth, add flour, salt, and ginger. Stir in the pecans.

4 Scrape half the batter into the prepared baking pan and place in the freezer for 30 minutes. Then spread the jam over the frozen batter, leaving about ½-inch around the edge. Spread the remaining batter over the top and bake for 45 minutes, or until a skewer comes out clean.

5 Cool completely on a wire rack before cutting.

Orange~Walnut Pumpkin Bars

MAKES 35
SMALL BARS *or*
20 LARGE BARS

When I bring these to a potluck, people always ask who made them and want the recipe. Crunchy on the top and bottom with a creamy spicy pumpkin filling perfumed with orange, this makes for a delightful morsel. I cut them small when serving as cookies, and large when serving on a plate for dessert.

CRUST

- ½ cup (1 stick) unsalted butter, softened
- 1 cup light brown sugar
- 1 cup unbleached all-purpose flour
- ½ cup whole wheat pastry flour
- 1 cup rolled oats
- ½ teaspoon salt

FILLING

- 1½ cups canned unsweetened pumpkin
- 1 cup nonfat evaporated milk
- ⅓ cup sugar
- 2 eggs
- 1 teaspoon grated orange zest
- 1 teaspoon cinnamon
- 1 teaspoon vanilla extract
- ½ teaspoon ground ginger
- ½ teaspoon salt
- ¼ teaspoon ground nutmeg
- ¼ teaspoon allspice
- 1½ cups finely chopped walnuts
- ⅓ cup shredded coconut (optional)
- Confectioners' sugar, for dusting

1 Heat the oven to 350°F.

2 To make the crust, beat the butter and sugar together in a large bowl. Stir in the flours, oats, and salt. When thoroughly combined and crumbly, remove about ¾ cup and set aside for the topping. Scrape the crumbs into a 10- by 14-inch jelly-roll pan, press flat with the palms of your hands, and bake for 10 minutes, or until lightly golden on the edges. Remove from oven and cool slightly on a wire rack.

3 Meanwhile, to make the filling, combine the pumpkin, milk, sugar, eggs, orange zest, cinnamon, vanilla, ginger, salt, allspice, and nutmeg in the same large bowl used for the crust. Spread the filling on the cooled crust. Mix the reserved crumbs with the walnuts and coconut, if desired, and sprinkle on top.

4 Bake for 30 to 35 minutes, or until lightly browned on the edges. Cool on a wire rack and sprinkle with confectioners' sugar. Cut in squares, large or small depending on the use.

White Chocolate, Pepita, and *Apricot Pumpkin Bars*

MAKES 24 SQUARES

These crunchy bar cookies are perfect for those allergic to nuts, and pretty wonderful for those who aren't.

CRUST

- 1 **cup unbleached all-purpose flour**
- 1 **cup brown sugar**
- ½ **teaspoon salt**
- ½ **cup (1 stick) cold butter, cut into small pieces, plus 2 tablespoons**
- 1½ **cups rolled oats**

TOPPING

- 2 **egg whites, slightly beaten**
- 1 **tablespoon cider vinegar**
- ½ **cup pepitas**
- ¾ **cup white chocolate chips**
- ½ **cup dried apricots, chopped**
- ¾ **cup pumpkin butter**

◆ ◆ ◆

Variation:
Try substituting chopped pecans or pistachios for pepitas and semi-sweet chocolate chips for the white chocolate ones.

◆ ◆ ◆

1 Heat the oven to 350°F.

2 Place the pepitas on a jelly-roll pan and toast in the oven for 2 to 3 minutes, or until they swell and pop. Cool on a rack.

3 Combine the flour, sugar, and salt in a food processor. Pulse once or twice to mix. Add ½ cup of the butter gradually, and pulse until crumbly. Add the oats and pulse once or twice. Remove 1¼ cup of this mixture and set aside.

4 Pat the remaining mixture into an ungreased 9- by 13-inch baking pan. Bake for 15 minutes, then cool on a wire rack for about 20 minutes.

5 While the crust is baking, melt the remaining 2 tablespoons of butter and whisk it together with the frothy egg whites, vinegar, pepitas, chocolate chips, apricots, and the reserved crumb mixture for the topping.

6 Spread the pumpkin butter over the cooled crust, leaving a small ¼-inch border. Evenly spread the topping over the pumpkin butter.

7 Bake for 30 minutes, or until lightly browned and bubbly. Cool completely on a wire rack before cutting into squares.

CAKES

Homemade cakes are always special. Served at the end of a meal or with coffee, a homemade cake says "I care!" Even if it is relatively easy to make, as are most of the cakes in this chapter, your friends and family will appreciate your effort. Pumpkin adds moisture to these cakes and makes them richly delicious and, of course, beautifully colorful.

Following the recipes is important in making cakes because by balancing the ingredients, certain chemical reactions occur that allow the cake to rise and brown properly. If you change ingredients, or the quantities, you may find yourself with a soggy mess. I don't mean to discourage creativity, but at least follow the recipe exactly the first time you make it, and then if you want to invent, try changing the spice mix, which changes the flavor but won't change the chemistry.

CANNED UNSWEETENED *Pumpkin*

Canned unsweetened pumpkin is often sold side by side with pumpkin pie filling, which contains sugar and spices and is ready to pop into a prepared piecrust. The recipes in this book are for the unsweetened variety, and I don't recommend substituting even if you are making a pie.

Gingerbread with Pumpkin
Ice Cream and Caramel Sauce

MAKES ONE
9- X 9-INCH CAKE

My friend Wendy, a California caterer, suggested the combination for this fabulous dessert.

- 1 cup canned unsweetened pumpkin
- ½ cup buttermilk
- ½ cup molasses
- 1 egg
- 4 tablespoons unsalted butter, melted
- 2 cups unbleached all-purpose flour
- ½ cup sugar
- 1 tablespoon peeled and grated fresh ginger
- 1 teaspoon baking soda
- ½ teaspoon salt
- 1 teaspoon ground cinnamon
- ½ teaspoon ground allspice
- 1 quart Ginger-Pumpkin Ice Cream (see page 182)
- 1½ cups Caramel Sauce (see page 183, or use store bought)

1 Heat the oven to 350°F. Spray a 9- by 9-inch baking pan with cooking spray.

2 Combine the pumpkin, buttermilk, molasses, egg, and melted butter in a large bowl.

3 Sift the flour, sugar, ginger, baking soda, salt, cinnamon, and allspice into the pumpkin mixture and stir to combine.

4 Pour the batter into the prepared baking pan and bake for 25 to 35 minutes, or until a skewer into the center comes out clean. Cool in the pan on a wire rack. When completely cool, cut into 12 generous servings.

5 Serve each piece with a dollop of the ice cream. Spoon Caramel Sauce over both and serve with a flourish.

Ginger-Pumpkin Ice Cream

MAKES 1 QUART   *Ginger loves pumpkin in this frosty mix, providing a burst of flavor.*

1 quart creamy French vanilla ice cream, slightly softened

1 cup canned unsweetened pumpkin

½ cup brown sugar

1 teaspoon ground ginger

1 tablespoon minced crystallized ginger

¼ teaspoon ground nutmeg

1 Thoroughly mix the pumpkin, sugar, ground and crystallized ginger, and nutmeg together.

2 Fold in the ice cream until the mixture is all one color. Pack it in a freezer container and store in the freezer. Allow the ice cream to soften slightly before serving.

Pumpkin-Orange Cheesecake
Surprising

I could not resist the inspiration for the crust of this truly unique cheesecake, which comes from the pages of Martha Storey and Friends' 500 Treasured Country Recipes. A traditional cheesecake filling is nestled in a surprising crust made from almonds, gingersnap crumbs, and pumpkin for a wonderfully unusual cheesecake experience. The filling is my old favorite from the Statler Hotel at Cornell University.

SERVES 10

CRUST

- 1 pound fresh pumpkin, seeds and fibers removed, unpeeled and grated (about 3 cups)
- 15 gingersnaps, rolled into crumbs (about ¾ cups)
- ½ cup almonds, finely chopped
- 2 tablespoons sugar
- 1 teaspoon grated orange zest
- 1 tablespoon butter, melted

FILLING

- 4 packages (8-ounces each) cream cheese, softened
- 4 eggs
- 1 tablespoon freshly squeezed lemon juice
- 1 teaspoon vanilla extract
- 1 cup sugar

1 Heat the oven to 350°F. Grease a 9-inch springform pan with butter.

2 To make the crust, combine the pumpkin, crumbs, almonds, sugar and orange zest in a medium bowl. Add the butter and mix well.

3 Cover the bottom of the prepared pan with the mixture and press down lightly with a fork. Bake for 30 minutes. Cool on a wire rack.

4 Increase the oven temperature to 450°F.

5 To make the filling, beat the cream cheese in a stand mixer or with a hand mixer. Add the eggs, one at a time, beating after each addition. Next, beat in the lemon juice and vanilla. Add the sugar and beat only until it is dissolved into the mixture.

6 Pour the cream cheese mixture into the cooled crust, and bake for only 30 to 35 minutes, until set, but with a jiggle in the center. Turn off the oven and cool the cheesecake in the oven. Chill before serving.

Pumpkin Roll
with Mascarpone Filling

Not only does this dessert have a fabulous blend of flavors, but it is also a beauty to behold and a fitting ending to a meal for your favorite people. To toast the almonds, spread them on a baking sheet and put in a 350°F oven for 3 to 5 minutes, or until fragrant and light brown.

SERVES 12

CAKE

- 4 eggs
- ¾ cup sugar
- ¾ cup canned unsweetened pumpkin
- ¾ cup unbleached all-purpose flour
- 1 teaspoon ground cinnamon
- ½ teaspoon ground ginger
- ½ teaspoon salt
- ¼ teaspoon ground cloves

FILLING

- 2 containers (8 ounces) mascarpone cheese, at room temperature
- ¼ cup confectioners' sugar, plus 2 tablespoons
- 2 tablespoons crystallized ginger
- 1 teaspoon vanilla extract

1 Heat the oven to 350°F. Line a 15- by 10-inch jelly-roll pan with parchment paper.

2 Beat the eggs on high speed until thick and lemon-colored, about 5 minutes with a hand mixer, 3 minutes with a stand mixer. Gradually beat in the sugar and then stir in the pumpkin.

3 Sift the flour, cinnamon, ginger, salt, and cloves into the egg mixture, and fold into the egg mixture until the flour is completely incorporated. Evenly spread the batter in the prepared pan.

4 Bake for 15 to 20 minutes, or until springy when lightly touched. Cool completely on a wire rack. While the cake is cooling, mix the mascarpone, confectioners' sugar, ginger, and vanilla together in a small bowl. Set aside.

5 Sprinkle a tea towel with the remaining 2 tablespoons of confectioners' sugar. Carefully invert the cake onto the towel. Peel the parchment paper from the cake.

⅓ cup sliced almonds, toasted
Caramel Sauce (see below)

6 Spread the filling mixture over the entire cake, leaving about ½-inch around the edges. Begin rolling at the narrow edge by lifting the towel and roll as tightly as you can. The cake is quite fragile and may break slightly while rolling. Persevere, as the filling will help hold it together. Trim the edges with a serrated knife.

7 Place the roll on a long platter, seam-side down. With a serrated knife, cut into ¾-inch slices. Drizzle the warm caramel sauce on each slice, and sprinkle with some almonds for a spectacular dessert.

Caramel Sauce

MAKES 1½ CUPS

1 cup sugar

¼ cup water

2 tablespoons light corn syrup

1 cup heavy cream

2 tablespoons unsalted butter

1 teaspoon vanilla extract

Pinch salt

1 Combine sugar, water, and corn syrup in a medium heavy-bottomed saucepan. Bring to a boil over medium-high heat. Dip a pastry brush in the water and wash the sugar crystals down the sides of the pan. Boil for 9 to 10 minutes, or until the sugar turns an amber color. Do not stir.

2 This mixture will be very hot. Remove the pan from heat and pour in the heavy cream, being careful not to let it splatter on you. Return to the heat and bring to a boil. Stir in the butter. Remove from heat once more. Stir in the vanilla and salt.

3 This sauce will keep at room temperature for several days. For longer storage, pour it into a glass jar and refrigerate. When ready to use, place the jar in a small saucepan with an inch of water. Gently heat until the sauce warms up and is pourable.

Pumpkin Cheesecake with Graham and Zweiback Crust

Cheesecake is a dessert of a thousand variations. It is rich, it is fattening, and to eat a slice is a sensory experience. In searching for the perfect cheesecake, texture is what it is all about for me. The smoothest and creamiest ones are always the best, and pumpkin enhances both. In this version, the mild pumpkin flavor, perfumed with spices, enriches the total experience.

Zweiback crackers are found with the baby foods in a supermarket. They come in a 6-ounce box with 2 packages inside. They are old-fashioned teething crackers.

SERVES 12

CRUST

- 4 zweiback crackers, broken and processed into crumbs
- 4 whole graham crackers, broken and processed into crumbs
- 1 tablespoon sugar
- ½ teaspoon ground cinnamon
- ½ teaspoon ground ginger
- 2 tablespoons unsalted butter, melted

1 Heat the oven to 325°F and spray the bottom and sides of a 9-inch springform pan with butter-flavored cooking spray.

2 To make the crust, combine the zweiback crumbs, graham cracker crumbs, sugar, cinnamon, and ginger. Mix in the butter with your hands. Press the mixture into the prepared pan, about ½-inch up the side, using the palm of your hand or a flat-bottomed glass to make it flat. Bake for 15 minutes, until slightly browned at edges. Cool on a wire rack while you make the filling.

3 Bring a kettle full of water to a boil over high heat.

4 To make the filling, cook the pumpkin for 5 to 7 minutes in a nonstick skillet over low heat, stirring occasionally to remove some of the moisture.

5 While the pumpkin is cooking, beat the cream cheese until smooth in a standing mixer at medium speed or

FILLING

- 2 cups canned unsweetened pumpkin
- 3 packages cream cheese (8 ounces each), cut into chunks and softened
- 1 cup sugar
- 1 teaspoon ground cinnamon
- 1 teaspoon ground ginger
- ¼ teaspoon ground allspice
- ¼ teaspoon ground cloves
- ¼ teaspoon ground nutmeg
- ½ teaspoon salt
- 1 tablespoon freshly squeezed lemon juice
- 1 teaspoon grated lemon zest
- 1 teaspoon vanilla extract
- 4 eggs
- ½ cup heavy cream

with a hand mixer at high speed. Mix the sugar with the cinnamon, ginger, allspice, cloves, nutmeg and salt in a small bowl and slowly beat into the cheese.

6 When the pumpkin is finished cooking, cool it slightly and add the lemon juice, zest, and vanilla.

7 Add the pumpkin mixture to the cream cheese mixture and beat at medium speed, just until blended.

8 Add the eggs one at a time, beating a little between each one at low speed. Finally, add the heavy cream and beat at low speed until the mixture is smooth and creamy. Do not overbeat.

9 Pour the batter into the prepared pan. Set a roasting pan on a shelf in the bottom third of the oven and pour the boiling kettle water into it to a level of 1-inch. Place the cheesecake on the shelf above and bake it in this modified boiling-water bath until the edges are set, but the center is still wobbly, about 1 hour.

10 Let the cheesecake and the boiling-water pan cool slightly in oven. Remove the cheesecake pan from oven and place on a wire rack away from drafts. Remove the roasting pan and discard the water. Run a knife around the edge of the cheesecake pan and remove the sides. Cool completely and then refrigerate. Bring to room temperature before serving.

Pumpkin Bundt Cake

good bundt cake is like a good piecrust. The ingredients are simple, but how you put them together is everything. This buttery cake is wonderful with tea or coffee, or to end a fine meal. To make a more elaborate dessert, add pumpkin ice cream and sprinkle with minced candied ginger.

**MAKES ONE
9-INCH CAKE**

1 cup (2 sticks) unsalted butter, softened

2 cups granulated sugar

1 teaspoon grated orange zest

4 eggs, at room temperature

1 cup canned unsweetened pumpkin

1 teaspoon vanilla extract

3 cups cake flour

2 teaspoons baking powder

½ teaspoon salt

Confectioners' sugar, for dusting

NOTE: A stand mixer is a big help in mixing this cake. I have made it with a hand mixer, but if you have a stand mixer, use it and avoid standing around. The results are the same, but it is just easier.

1 Heat the oven to 350°F. Butter a 9-inch, high-sided bundt pan. Sprinkle lightly with flour.

2 Beat the butter in a large bowl at medium speed for about 1 minute. Add the granulated sugar and orange zest and continue beating until pale in color, about 3 to 4 minutes. It will be grainy, but rather fluffy.

3 Add one egg at a time, beating on low. When an egg is mixed in, add the next one. Continuing on low speed, beat in the pumpkin and vanilla.

4 Sift the flour, baking powder, and salt into the bowl. At low speed, beat the mixture, scraping the sides of the bowl often, until the flour is almost mixed in. Use the scraper to fold the mixture and incorporate the last bit of flour into the batter.

5 Pour the batter into the prepared pan. Bake for 1 hour and 10 minutes, or until a skewer inserted into the center comes out clean and the top is golden brown.

6 Cool for 15 minutes on a wire rack before removing from the pan. Cool the cake completely on a wire rack, then lightly sift confectioners' sugar over the top. Place on a pretty cake plate and admire before slicing and serving.

Chocolate-Pumpkin Cake

A well-kept secret about this deliciously moist chocolate cake is that it is actually healthful! Don't tell, but the pumpkin packs in vitamins as well as a subtle flavor. Serve with whipped cream, ice cream, or a glass of ice-cold milk. Smile as you watch this cake disappear.

½ cup (1 stick) unsalted butter

3 ounces unsweetened baking chocolate

1 cup granulated sugar

½ cup light brown sugar

2 eggs, slightly beaten

1 cup canned unsweetened pumpkin

1 cup unbleached all-purpose flour

1 teaspoon ground cinnamon

½ teaspoon baking soda

½ teaspoon salt

¼ teaspoon baking powder

1 cup chopped walnuts (optional)

1 Heat the oven to 350°F. Spray a 9- by 13-inch baking pan with cooking spray.

2 Melt the butter and chocolate in a large heavy-bottomed 4-quart saucepan over low heat. Remove from the heat and add the sugars, stirring until totally blended. Beat in the eggs and pumpkin.

3 Sift the flour, cinnamon, baking soda, salt, and baking powder into the chocolate mixture and stir until all the flour is incorporated. Mix in the nuts, if using, and spread the batter in the prepared pan.

4 Bake for 30 minutes, or until the cake leaves the side of the pan and a skewer inserted in the center comes out clean. Cool on a rack.

Pumpkin Cake or
Jack~o'~Lantern Cake

Wow the kids with a bright orange pumpkin cake. Using the Chocolate-Pumpkin Cake recipe (see page 189), bake the cake in two round 8-inch cake pans. Cool for 10 minutes and remove from pans. Cool completely before icing.

ORANGE ICING

- 1 **package cream cheese (8 ounces), softened**
- 4 **tablespoons unsalted butter, softened**
- 1 **pound confectioners' sugar (about 4 cups)**
- 2 **tablespoons grated orange zest**
- 1 **tablespoon freshly squeezed orange juice**
  - **Orange food coloring**
  - **Green food coloring**
  - **Licorice strings**
  - **Candy corn**

1 Beat the cream cheese and butter in a medium bowl. Gradually sift in the sugar, and then add the orange zest and juice. Reserve 2 tablespoons of the icing. Add orange food coloring to the rest, until the icing is the color of a pumpkin. Add the green food coloring to the reserved icing.

2 Place one layer upside-down on a large plate, and put a thin layer of pumpkin-colored icing on it. Put the second layer on top. Trim the cakes with a serrated knife to make it somewhat pumpkin-shaped. Ice the top and sides with the pumpkin-colored icing. Put a blob of green icing off-center of the top for the stem. With a toothpick, lightly mark lines radiating from the stem to resemble pumpkin ridges. With licorice, create a jack-o'-lantern face on one side. Surround with candy corn and serve to a happy crowd of little goblins.

Halloween Party
for Little Ghosts and Goblins

"WHAT ARE YOU GOING TO BE on Halloween?" is heard in school hallways and playgrounds from the beginning of October to the exciting culmination on All Hallows Eve. I love the littlest ones who come to the door in bewilderment of what they are supposed to be and do. In a few years they know exactly as they hide behind their masks and costumes, ready to get a treat. My favorites are the slightly older kids who have created a clever costume, which they proudly display. I remember the group of girls who appeared at our door as crayons. To satisfy your yen for creating Halloween delectables, have a party for the kids.

If you really plan ahead and have a garden, you can carve the names of your favorite children on pumpkins while they are still in the patch and small in size. Use a sharp knife to cut through the skin only. The name will grow with the pumpkin over the summer and by Halloween each child will have a personalized pumpkin.

TABLE DECORATION

Get a bright orange plastic cloth to cover the table. In the center place a large glass container. Set a small vase filled with water in the container. Arrange some fall colored mums in the vase. Fill the space between the vase and the container with Halloween M & Ms. Put some small pumpkins and gourds around the container.

PUMPKIN CARVING AND DECORATING

Begin the carving activity with a Pumpkin Hunt. Hide pumpkins of all sizes around the yard or in the house, and let the kids find their jack-o'-lantern for carving. For the little kids, use small pumpkins. Instead of carving, have a good supply of washable markers. Be sure the pumpkins are washed and thoroughly dried before letting the kids loose with the markers. Basically match the size of the child with the size of the pumpkin.

For older children, pumpkin carving kits work well and supervision is a good idea. Whether to use templates or have the children create their own designs is up to you. Magazines in October abound with carving ideas and templates. There are even artificial pumpkins you can carve instead of fresh.

Putting a small flashlight inside the pumpkin while carving lets the carver see how the face will look as the carving proceeds. Cutting a hole in the bottom instead of the top will make it easier on the carver. You can then set the pumpkin over a flashlight or other light.

Kids' Menu

*H*ave food that is either orange, contains pumpkin or looks like a pumpkin.

*Tex-Mex Chili in a Pumpkin

* Punkin' Joes

Baby carrot sticks

*Jack-o'-Lantern Cookies

*Jack-o'-Lantern Cake

*Maple-Pumpkin Pops
with Lemon Icing

Orange Sherbet

Individual Pumpkin Pizzas
for the Little Kids

Flour tortillas

Grated orange Cheddar cheese

Sliced black olives

Tomato sauce in a squeeze bottle

Green bell pepper slices

Heat the oven to 400°F. Place several tortillas on a baking sheet. Spread a thin layer of sauce on each pizza, cover with cheese, and let each child make a face using olives, peppers, and squirts of sauce. Bake for 10 to 15 minutes, or until the cheese melts. Cool slightly and serve.

Spice Cake with Pumpkin
Mascarpone Icing

Not only does pumpkin in the frosting give a luscious peachy color to this cake, it provides a subtle contrast to the sweetness of the frosting and the spice of the cake. Little kids love this cake, and so do grown-ups.

- 1 cup light brown sugar
- ½ cup granulated sugar
- 2 eggs
- ½ cup canola oil
- 1 cup canned unsweetened pumpkin
- 2 cups unbleached all-purpose flour
- 2 teaspoons ground cinnamon
- 1 teaspoon ground allspice
- 1 teaspoon baking powder
- ½ teaspoon baking soda
- ½ teaspoon salt
- ⅔ cup buttermilk
- ½ cup walnuts, chopped

FROSTING

- 6 ounces mascarpone cheese
- 2 tablespoons unsalted butter, softened
- ⅓ cup canned unsweetened pumpkin
- 2 cups confectioners' sugar

1 Heat the oven to 350°F. Spray a 9- by 13-inch baking pan with cooking spray.

2 Combine the sugars in a large bowl. Beat in the eggs and slowly add the oil. Continue beating for several minutes, until fluffy, and then add the pumpkin.

3 Sift the flour, cinnamon, allspice, baking powder, baking soda, and salt into the pumpkin batter. Beat at low speed and add the buttermilk. Continue beating until the flour is thoroughly incorporated into the batter. Fold in the walnuts.

4 Pour the batter into the prepared pan. Bake for 40 to 45 minutes, or until the edges pull away from the sides and are slightly browned. Cool completely on a wire rack.

5 While cake is cooling, make the frosting. Mix the cheese and butter together in a bowl with a spoon. Add the pumpkin and gradually mix in the confectioners' sugar. When the cake is cool, spread the frosting.

6 Cut the cake into 2-inch squares and store in the refrigerator for up to a week, or chill, cover in plastic wrap, put in a freezer bag, and freeze for up to 2 months. Of course, it is best eaten while fresh.

Pumpkin~Carrot Cake with Orange Cream Cheese Frosting

Carrot cake is an all-time favorite. We might feel somewhat virtuous eating a big slice, because we are eating our vegetables. Think how good you will feel knowing there is also pumpkin enriching this classic.

CAKE

- 2 cups unbleached all-purpose flour
- 1 cup sugar
- 2 teaspoons baking soda
- 1 teaspoon ground cinnamon
- ½ teaspoon salt
- ¾ cup canola oil
- 4 eggs
- 1 cup canned unsweetened pumpkin
- 3 large carrots, peeled and grated (about 3 cups)
- 1 cup chopped walnuts
- ½ cup raisins

ORANGE CREAM CHEESE FROSTING

- 1 package (3 ounces) cream cheese, softened
- 2 tablespoons unsalted butter, softened
- 2 tablespoons orange juice
- 1 tablespoon orange zest
- 3 cups sifted confectioners' sugar

1 Heat the oven to 325°F. Spray a 9- by 13-inch baking pan with cooking spray.

2 To make the cake, sift the flour, sugar, baking soda, cinnamon, and salt into a large bowl. Mix the oil, eggs, pumpkin, and carrots in a small bowl, until blended. Stir into the flour mixture and stir to combine. Fold in the nuts and raisins.

3 Pour the batter into the prepared pan and bake for 35 to 40 minutes, or until a skewer inserted in the center comes out clean. Cool completely on a wire rack before frosting.

4 To make the frosting, thoroughly blend the cream cheese and butter. Beat in the orange juice, orange zest, and the confectioners' sugar. Continue beating until smooth. Spread over the cooled cake.

DESSERTS *and* DELICACIES

From spectacular Baked Alaska to creamy puddings to humble fudge, this chapter offers a variety of sweet choices for ending a meal. Pumpkin colors these desserts with a pale orange hue. Its flavor blends wonderfully with sugar and spice, and its smooth texture is a perfect addition to creamy puddings and many sweet concoctions.

Pumpkin Baked Alaska
with Pumpkin Ice Cream

This spectacular dessert consists of many parts, but the good news is that most of them can be prepared ahead. It requires last minute work for perfecting the meringue. That is when your guests are relaxing around the table enjoying each other's company while others are helping to clear the table. Inspiration for this recipe comes from Susan Carr's elaborate prize winning recipe at the Half Moon Bay Pumpkin Cooking Contest. Make the lovely cake or buy a nice round 1-inch high sponge cake.

SERVES 12

CAKE

- 3 eggs, separated
- 7 tablespoons sugar
- 1 tablespoon cake flour
- 1 cup pecans, finely ground
- ⅛ teaspoon cream of tartar
  Pinch of salt

FILLING

- 1½ quarts pumpkin ice cream
- 4 bars (1.4 ounces) English toffee candy, chopped

1 To make the cake, heat the oven to 350°F. Grease a 9-by 9-inch cake pan. Line with a circle of waxed paper, also greased.

2 To make the cake, place the yolks in a large bowl and the whites in a medium bowl. Beat the yolks with an electric mixer on medium speed or a hand mixer on high speed until thick and pale yellow, about 5 minutes. Gradually add 6 tablespoons of the sugar to the beaten yolks, beating until the mixture is light and fluffy. Mix the flour with the nuts and fold into the egg mixture. The batter will be thick and stiff.

3 Beat the egg whites with clean beaters until foamy. Add the cream of tartar and salt and continue beating, until soft peaks form. Slowly add the remaining tablespoon of sugar and continue beating until the whites are stiff but not dry.

4 Stir a third of the egg white mixture into the batter. Fold in the remaining whites, to make a light and airy batter. Spoon the batter into the prepared pan and bake

MERINGUE

- 5 egg whites, room temperature
- ¼ teaspoon cream of tartar
- ¼ teaspoon salt
- ½ cup superfine sugar (if unavailable, pulse granulated sugar in a food processor)
- 1 teaspoon vanilla extract

BEATING EGGWHITES

Be sure the bowl and beaters are clean and the whites at room temperature for best results. If you don't have time to let the eggs reach room temperature, set them in a bowl of warm water before separating.

A sure way to tell if egg whites are sufficiently beaten is to gradually turn the bowl upside down. If they start slipping out, go back to beating. When they stay in a bowl that is turned completely upside-down, they are ready.

for 15 to 20 minutes, or until the cake springs back when lightly touched and is golden brown. Cool on a rack for 30 minutes before removing from the pan.

5 Remove the cooled cake from the pan, peel off the waxed paper, and wrap in heavy-duty aluminum foil to store in the freezer until it is time to assemble the dessert. This cake can be made up to a week ahead.

6 Grease a 2-quart mixing bowl (8-inch diameter) with butter and line it with plastic wrap that hangs over the edges. Pack the ice cream into the bowl and store in the freezer until ready to assemble your masterpiece.

7 To assemble the dessert, remove the cake and ice cream from the freezer. Unwrap the cake and sprinkle with the toffee candy, leaving ¼-inch around the edge. Lift the ice cream out of the bowl and invert it onto the cake. Rewrap the whole thing and freeze until just before ready to serve.

8 For the final assembly, heat the oven to 500°F. Make the meringue by beating the egg whites in a large bowl with clean beaters until foamy. Add the cream of tartar and salt and continue beating on high, until soft peaks form. Slowly add the sugar, 1 tablespoon at a time so the sugar can dissolve. Beat until thick and glossy, but not dry. Add the vanilla.

9 Remove the cake and ice cream from the freezer, unwrap, and place it on a heat-proof 10-inch serving plate. Completely cover the cake and the filling with the meringue and make a few swirls and peaks on the top with the back of a spoon. Place the dessert in the oven for 1 to 2 minutes, or until the meringue is lightly browned. Remove from oven and serve in luscious slices.

Lemon-Pumpkin Strudel

Traditional strudel made by German grandmothers with their sleeves pushed up is made of dough so thin you could read a newspaper through it. My German grandmother, however, would rather do anything but cook. This recipe, inspired by The Classic Zucchini Cookbook *and the strudel-making Omas, uses my favorite workhorse, phyllo dough, for the crust. Lemon brightens the pumpkin, giving it the tang of tart apples in this fairly simple version of strudel. Serve with vanilla or cinnamon-flavored ice cream, or just as it is.*

SERVES 8

1 pound fresh pumpkin, seeds and fibers removed, peeled and grated (about 2½ cups)

¼ cup freshly squeezed lemon juice

¼ cup water

⅓ cup brown sugar

3 teaspoons ground cinnamon

1 teaspoon fresh lemon zest

¼ teaspoon ground nutmeg

2 tablespoons granulated sugar

6 sheets phyllo dough, thawed

4 tablespoons unsalted butter, melted

½ cup walnuts, finely chopped

10–12 amaretti cookies, ground into crumbs

1 Heat the oven to 400°F.

2 Bring the pumpkin, lemon juice, and water to a boil in medium saucepan over medium heat. Reduce heat and simmer for about 10 minutes, until the pumpkin is tender, but not mushy.

3 Stir in the brown sugar, 2 teaspoons of the cinnamon, lemon zest, and nutmeg into the pumpkin mixture and set aside.

4 Mix together the remaining teaspoon cinnamon with the granulated sugar in a small bowl and set aside.

5 Place a sheet of phyllo on a clean surface, brush with the melted butter, and sprinkle with a little cinnamon and sugar. Set a second sheet on top of the first, brush with butter, and sprinkle with cinnamon and sugar. Repeat until you have a stack of six phyllo leaves.

6 Combine the walnuts and amaretti crumbs and sprinkle over the top. Spread the pumpkin mixture on top of the crumbs, leaving a 1-inch border around the edges. Fold the long edges over the filling and, starting at the narrow end, tightly roll the strudel. Place on a baking sheet, seam-side down, and brush with the remaining butter.

7 Bake for 25 minutes, or until golden brown on the top. Place the pan on a wire rack and cool. Slice into thick rounds and serve warm or at room temperature.

NOTE: To make the amaretti crumbs, place the cookies in a plastic bag and whack them with a rolling pin. They crumble very easily.

Phyllo

Phyllo is very thin sheets of pastry typically used in Greek and Mediterranean cooking. You will find it in the freezer case of the supermarket in a long, thin box. The sheets are carefully wrapped and sealed. Thaw it before opening the package. When opening the package, have a slightly damp tea towel on hand to cover the opened package as you work. Lift each sheet on the work surface and proceed with the recipe.

Pumpkin Mousse
in Phyllo Cups

A mellow, creamy mousse nestled in crisp, buttery cups is deceptively simple to make. Make in regular muffin cups for dessert or in mini cups to be part of a dessert plate.

SERVES 8

3 sheets phyllo dough, thawed (see page 199)

Butter-flavored cooking spray

1 cup canned unsweetened pumpkin

3 tablespoons brown sugar

2 tablespoons pure maple syrup

1 tablespoon freshly squeezed lemon juice

1 tablespoon minced crystallized ginger

½ teaspoon ground cinnamon

¼ teaspoon ground allspice

½ cup heavy cream, whipped to soft peaks

4 amaretti cookies, crushed

8 mint leaves

1 Heat the oven to 350°F.

2 Stack the 3 sheets of phyllo on top of each other. Cut into eight 4-inch squares.

3 Tuck each stack of squares into a muffin cup. Spray each phyllo cup with cooking spray, making sure to spray the insides and the tops. Bake for 6 to 7 minutes. Cool cups on a wire rack.

4 To make the mousse, combine the pumpkin, brown sugar, maple syrup, lemon juice, ginger, cinnamon, and allspice in a medium bowl. Fold in the whipped heavy cream. Spoon the mousse into the phyllo cups just before serving. Sprinkle each with a little bit of crushed amaretti cookies and serve with a tiny mint leaf tucked into each cup.

Almond Bread Pudding
with Crème Anglaise

Bread pudding is the epitome of "Waste not, Want not" thinking, and the perfect use for leftover tasty bread. A crispy top over a creamy interior tinged with maple and almond makes this a true comfort food. Serve plain or create a sublime dessert by topping it with a simple Crème Anglaise, my all-time favorite sauce.

SERVES 8

4 **cups day-old sourdough bread, cut into 1-inch cubes**

4 **eggs, slightly beaten**

2 **cups half-and-half**

1 **cup evaporated nonfat milk**

1 **cup canned unsweetened pumpkin**

½ **cup sugar**

¼ **cup pure maple syrup**

¼ **teaspoon almond extract**

¼ **teaspoon ground nutmeg**

¼ **teaspoon salt**

¼ **cup toasted sliced almonds**

◆ ◆ ◆

Variation:

Instead of using sourdough bread, use leftover pumpkin bread in this recipe. Skip the canned pumpkin and almonds and proceed with the instructions.

◆ ◆ ◆

1 Grease a 2-quart casserole dish with butter. Place the bread in a large bowl.

2 Combine the eggs, half-and-half, milk, pumpkin, sugar, maple syrup, almond extract, nutmeg, and salt in another bowl. Pour over the bread and let sit for 30 minutes. It could sit out longer and even overnight, in which case, store covered in the refrigerator. Bring to room temperature before cooking.

3 Heat the oven to 350°F and set a tea kettle full of water to boil.

4 Pour the bread and egg mixture into the prepared casserole dish and sprinkle with the almonds. Set the dish in a large roasting pan in the oven. Pour the boiling water to a depth of 1-inch in the roasting pan, surrounding the casserole dish. This boiling-water bath will allow the custard to cook gently, giving the creamy result that makes bread pudding so satisfying.

5 Bake for 40 to 45 minutes. The custard should be a little soupy. Remove from the oven and take the casserole out of the hot water and let it cool. Serve at room temperature, or chill in the refrigerator before serving.

Crème Anglaise

Also known as stirred custard or custard sauce, this is one of those simple recipes in which method is everything.

4 egg yolks

⅓ cup sugar

½ cup whole milk

1 teaspoon vanilla extract

1 Whisk the egg yolks and sugar together in a medium bowl.

2 Heat the milk in a medium saucepan over medium heat until little bubbles form around the edge. Stir, so as not to burn the milk.

3 Pour the hot milk into the egg mixture, whisking all the time. Pour this back into the saucepan. Cook over medium-low heat, stirring constantly with a flat-bottomed wooden spoon until the mixture thickens slightly, to the consistency of heavy cream. Remove from the heat and stir in vanilla.

4 Pour the sauce through a sieve back into the medium bowl and chill in the refrigerator. When completely cold, pour the sauce into a pitcher and cover. Pour some cold sauce over each serving of warm bread pudding.

5 The sauce will keep for 3 days in the refrigerator. Enrich a bowl of fresh berries with a splash of leftover sauce.

Pumpkin-Rice Pudding

I have always thought that soft, creamy rice was the best kind of pudding, and when lightly flavored and colored with pumpkin, spice, and citrus, it becomes divine.

SERVES 8

5 cups whole milk

½ cup arborio rice

½ cup canned unsweetened pumpkin

⅓ cup sugar

1 cinnamon stick

¼ teaspoon salt

⅓ cup raisins (optional)

1 egg

1 teaspoon finely grated lemon zest

1 teaspoon vanilla extract

TIP: The best spoon for stirring this pudding is a flat-bottomed wooden one. With each swipe of the spoon, you can cover much more of the bottom of the pot than with the tip of a regular wooden spoon.

1 Heat the milk, rice, pumpkin, sugar, cinnamon stick, and salt in a large heavy-bottomed saucepan over medium heat, stirring occasionally, until tiny bubbles form around the edge of the pan and steam rises.

2 Reduce heat to low and gently cook, uncovered, for about 45 to 50 minutes, or until the rice is tender and the pudding thick, but still soupy. Stir frequently, especially towards the end of the cooking time, when the mixture thickens. Add the raisins, if using, in the last 10 minutes of cooking. If possible, put a heat diffuser under the pot to keep the heat evenly distributed and to prevent scorching the milk, something you definitely don't want to do.

3 Beat the egg with a fork in a small bowl. Spoon some of the pudding into the egg. Slowly add this egg mixture to the pudding, stirring constantly and keeping the heat low. Cook for 1 to 2 minutes, or until the pudding thickens some more.

4 Remove from heat, stir in the lemon zest and vanilla, and cool slightly before thoroughly chilling. Remove the cinnamon stick and serve in dessert dishes.

Orange~Pumpkin Spanish Cream

SERVES 6

My mother used to make Spanish cream as a special treat. I always loved its eggy smoothness and find it better than ever with orange, pumpkin, and spices. The pumpkin adds a subtle flavor and a lovely color to this fine traditional pudding. My mom had some old individual metal molds that she used for Spanish cream. Each was a different shape and all were somewhat battered, which only added to their charm. I'm sure they could be found in antique shops or in flea markets.

1 package (.25 ounce) unflavored gelatin (about 1 tablespoon)

¼ cup cold orange juice

2 cups whole milk

3 eggs, separated

⅔ cup sugar

½ cup canned unsweetened pumpkin

¼ teaspoon grated orange zest

¼ teaspoon ground allspice

Pinch of salt

1 Dissolve the gelatin in the orange juice and set aside.

2 Heat the milk in a medium-sized heavy-bottomed saucepan over medium-low heat, until tiny bubbles form around the edge, about 3 to 5 minutes. Do not let it boil.

3 Beat the egg yolks in a small bowl with the sugar, pumpkin, orange zest, allspice, and salt. Add about ½ cup of the hot milk, stirring while adding. Return the egg mixture to the hot milk, stirring constantly. Cook over medium-low heat until mixture coats a flat-bottomed wooden spoon, about 5 minutes. Be careful not to let it boil. Stir constantly while the custard is cooking. Cool the mixture and stir in the gelatin.

4 Beat the egg whites until foamy. Continue beating until they form peaks and when you tilt the bowl, they do not slide toward the edge. When beaten enough, they will be shiny and not dry.

5 Add a heaping spoon of egg whites to the pumpkin mixture and stir to combine. Fold the remaining egg whites into pumpkin mixture. It will become foamy.

6 Rinse a 1-quart mold with cold water and pour the pudding into the mold or into a pretty serving dish. Chill for at least 3 hours, until set. Unmold the pudding onto a large plate and serve in dessert bowls.

EGG WHITE *Safety*

You will notice that the egg whites are not cooked. If you are confident that your eggs do not carry salmonella, it is okay to proceed with this recipe as written. If you are concerned, use powdered egg whites, following the instructions on the package for beating them. I much prefer to use fresh eggs that I feel are safe. Egg whites from pasteurized eggs are not recommended for whipping.

Pumpkin Panna Cotta

udy Witts introduced me to this classic light Italian dessert of sweetened "cooked cream" in her cooking class in Florence, Italy. It lends itself to many variations. Perfumed with cardamom and flavored with pumpkin, it not only tastes wonderful, but also gives a lovely three-tiered look to the traditionally pale-colored dessert.

SERVES 4

- 2 teaspoons (.25 ounces) unflavored gelatin
- ¼ cup cold water
- 2 cups whole milk
- ¼ cup sugar
- ¼ cup canned unsweetened pumpkin
- 1 teaspoon grated orange zest
- ¼ teaspoon ground cardamom
- 4 sprigs of mint

1 Stir the gelatin and water together in a small cup and set aside.

2 Heat the milk, sugar, and pumpkin together in a medium saucepan over medium-low heat, until small bubbles form around the edge. Do not let it boil. Stir occasionally to prevent scorching.

3 Remove pan from heat and stir in the gelatin, orange zest, and cardamom. Pour into four dessert dishes and let sit until the milk has cooled. Stir each dish and refrigerate for several hours.

4 Serve cold, garnished with a sprig of mint on each.

Peachy Pumpkin Crisp

Crisps speak of summer, but when fruits are out of season, this rich, spicy combination adds a hint of fall to our old favorite.

SERVES 6

⅓ cup canned unsweetened pumpkin

⅓ cup brown sugar

1 teaspoon grated lemon zest

½ teaspoon ground cinnamon

¼ teaspoon ground cloves

¼ teaspoon salt

1 can (29 ounces) peach halves, rinsed and well drained

TOPPING

½ cup rolled oats

⅓ cup brown sugar

¼ cup unbleached all-purpose flour

4 tablespoons unsalted butter

1 Heat the oven to 375°F. Grease a 2-quart casserole dish with butter.

2 Mix the pumpkin, sugar, lemon zest, cinnamon, cloves, and salt in a medium bowl. Add the peaches to the pumpkin mixture and place in the prepared casserole dish.

3 To make the topping, combine the oats, sugar, flour, and butter in a small bowl, using a pastry blender. The mixture should look crumbly. Scatter the crumbs on top of the peaches and bake for 25 to 30 minutes, or until bubbly.

4 Cool slightly and serve with coffee or ginger ice cream.

NOTE: If fresh peaches are in season, substitute 4 cling-free peaches, peeled and cut in half, for the canned peaches.

Frozen Pumpkin Dessert
with Nut Crust

This dessert has it all—a crunchy top and bottom, and a smooth, creamy, rich and spicy center. My friend Judy served a summer version of this dessert with strawberries to a crowd of houseguests, who all wanted the recipe. This fall and winter version is a great make-ahead dessert.

To drain the pumpkin, line a sieve with a folded paper towel and place the pumpkin on top. Shake the sieve a few times and, when the towel turns orange, replace it with another. Repeat this twice. This will remove some excess moisture and make the pumpkin more concentrated.

MAKES 24 PIECES

CRUST

- 1¼ cups unbleached all-purpose flour
- ½ cup unsalted butter, cold, cut into small pieces
- ½ cup brown sugar
- ¾ cup chopped pecans

1 Heat the oven to 350°F.

2 To make the crust, combine the flour, butter, and brown sugar with a pastry blender in a large bowl, or pulse in a food processor until the mixture resembles coarse crumbs. Add the nuts and spread on a jelly-roll pan. Bake 15 to 20 minutes until lightly browned, stirring every 5 minutes. Cool on a wire rack.

FILLING

- 3 egg whites, at room temperature
- ½ cup granulated sugar
- 1½ cups canned unsweetened pumpkin, drained
- ½ cup brown sugar
- 2 tablespoons pure maple syrup
- 2 tablespoons freshly squeezed lemon juice
- 1½ teaspoons ground cinnamon
- ¼ teaspoon ground nutmeg
- ¼ teaspoon salt
- 1 cup heavy cream

3 Meanwhile, to make the filling, beat the egg whites until stiff peaks form. Slowly add the granulated sugar and continue beating until the sugar is dissolved. Fold in the pumpkin, brown sugar, and maple syrup. Stir in the lemon juice, cinnamon, nutmeg, and salt.

4 Whip the cream to soft peaks and fold into the pumpkin mixture.

5 Spread half the crumb mixture in the bottom of a 9-by 13-inch baking pan. Cover with the pumpkin mixture. Top with the remaining crumbs, pressing into pumpkin slightly. Cover with aluminum foil and freeze for 3 to 4 hours, until firm. Set out for about 15 minutes before cutting and serving.

NOTE: This dessert may be kept in the freezer, well covered, for up to a week, if by any chance there is any left.

Pumpkin Ice Cream

This is a very quick way to create a luscious, creamy, spicy pumpkin ice cream. If you are into making your own from scratch, bless you and look elsewhere for a more complicated version. Be sure to use really good ice cream for this one. Don't soften the ice cream too much before mixing in the pumpkin because it will crystallize as it refreezes. Serve with Caramel Sauce (see page 183) and chopped cashews.

MAKES 1 QUART

1 cup canned unsweetened pumpkin

½ cup brown sugar

½ teaspoon ground cinnamon

½ teaspoon ground ginger

¼ teaspoon ground nutmeg

1 quart creamy French vanilla ice cream, slightly softened

1 Thoroughly mix the pumpkin, sugar, cinnamon, ginger, and nutmeg together.

2 Fold in the ice cream until the mixture is all one color.

3 Pack a freezer container and store in the freezer. Allow the ice cream to soften slightly before serving.

◆ ◆ ◆

Variation

For ginger–pumpkin ice cream, use 1 teaspoon ground ginger and 1 tablespoon minced crystallized ginger instead of the cinnamon and nutmeg.

◆ ◆ ◆

White Chocolate Pumpkin Fudge

MAKES 2 POUNDS

In Half Moon Bay, California, Denise Vidosit was kind enough to share the recipe for her wondrous creation. This fudge is in a class by itself.

1⅓ cups sugar

⅓ cup corn syrup

¼ cup water

⅓ cup canned unsweetened pumpkin, drained (see page 208 for instructions)

1 teaspoon ground cinnamon

¼ teaspoon ground cloves

¼ teaspoon ground ginger

¼ teaspoon ground mace or nutmeg

1 egg white

2¼ cups (15 ounces) white chocolate, chunks or chips

½ cup pecans, finely chopped

1 ounce dark chocolate

◆ ◆ ◆

Variation

Substitute 5 ounces of dark, sweet chocolate for the 5 ounces of the white chocolate to make a more chocolaty fudge.

◆ ◆ ◆

1 Stir the sugar, corn syrup, and water together in a medium heavy-bottomed saucepan, until well mixed. Cook over medium heat, without stirring, until the mixture reaches the soft-ball stage, 238°F on a candy thermometer, about 8 to 10 minutes. Dip a pastry brush in cold water and brush down the sides of the pan if crystals begin to form.

2 While the sugar water is heating, mix the pumpkin with the cinnamon, cloves, ginger, and mace in a small bowl and set aside.

3 Beat the egg white in a medium bowl until stiff peaks form. Very slowly, pour the hot sugar water into the egg whites, beating continuously until well combined.

4 Stir in the white chocolate until melted. Add the pumpkin mixture and beat until it begins to lose its glossiness, about 5 to 7 minutes. Stir in half of the pecans.

5 Grease an 8- by 8-inch pan with butter. Scrape the fudge into the prepared pan and let set for 5 minutes.

6 Melt the dark chocolate in a microwave on high for 30 seconds. Drizzle over the fudge and sprinkle with the remaining pecans. Let the fudge sit in the refrigerator for 1 hour before cutting into squares. Cover and store in the refrigerator.

Pumpkin Fudge

MAKES 1 POUND

Do not be fooled into thinking that all fudge must be chocolate. Here is a spicy version that is perfect for fall sugar cravings.

2 cups sugar

½ cup evaporated milk

3 tablespoons canned unsweetened pumpkin

½ teaspoon cinnamon

¼ teaspoon cornstarch

½ teaspoon vanilla extract

1 Grease a 9-inch square baking pan with butter.

2 Combine the sugar, milk, pumpkin, cinnamon, and cornstarch in a large saucepan. Cook over low heat, stirring constantly, until the mixture boils. Still stirring, continue to cook until the mixture reaches 236°F on a candy thermometer.

3 Remove from heat, add the vanilla, and beat with an electric mixer until the mixture is smooth. Scrape into the prepared pan and let cool.

4 When it is completely cooled, cut into squares and enjoy, or wrap carefully and store in the refrigerator for later.

◆ ◆ ◆

Variation

For an added treat, melt ½ cup semi-sweet chocolate chips in a microwave on high for 30 seconds. Drizzle the melted chocolate on top of the fudge in an irregular pattern.

◆ ◆ ◆

INDEX

Boldface entries indicate tables.

OTHER STOREY TITLES YOU WILL ENJOY

Apple Cookbook, by Olwen Woodier.
More than 140 recipes to put everyone's favorite fruit into tasty new combinations.
192 pages. Paper. ISBN-13: 978-1-58017-389-6.

The Classic Zucchini Cookbook, by Nancy C. Ralston,
Marynor Jordan, and Andrea Chesman.
A completely revised and updated edition that includes an illustrated primer to zucchini and squash, plus 225 recipes.
320 pages. Paper. ISBN-13 978-1-58017-453-4.

Maple Syrup Cookbook, by Ken Haedrich.
Recipes both sweet and savory that feature maple syrup and its wonderful earth, tangy qualities.
144 pages. Paper. ISBN-13: 978-1-58017-404-6.

Mom's Best Crowd-Pleasers, by Andrea Chesman.
A relaxed approach to feeding casual gathering of every size with little fuss.
208 pages. Paper. ISBN-13: 978-1-58017-629-3.

The Perfect Pumpkin, by Gale Damerow.
Detailed instructions on how to grow and harvest more then 95 varieties, plus craft projects and recipes.
224 pages. Paper. ISBN-13: 978-0-88266-993-9.

Serving Up the Harvest, by Andrea Chesman.
A collection of 175 recipes to bring out the best in garden-fresh vegetables, with 14 master recipes that can accommodate whatever happens to be in your produce basket.
516 pages. Paper. ISBN-13: 978-1-58017-663-7.

These and other books from Storey Publishing are available wherever quality books are sold or by calling 1-800-441-5700.
Visit us at *www.storey.com*.